PRAISE FOR *CLEAN DESIGN*

"Robin Wilson is a champion of wellness in the home. As a leading health advocate and d[...] helped many families learn about the seriousness of asthma and allergies and how our [...] or a help to good health. Asthma and allergy prevalence is growing, and avoiding allerger[...] and asthma triggers [...] the home can help."

—**Mike Tringale, MSM, Senior Vice President, External Affairs**
Asthma and Allergy Foundation of America

"As a physician who daily is consulted on the health of children and adults with allergies and sensitivities, I found this book inspiring. Robin Wilson uses her personal experiences and her incredible instinct to present us with a wonderful resource."

—**Dr. Joy L. Touchstone, MD**
Pediatrician

"Eco-healthy lifestyle expert and designer, Robin Wilson, has introduced an important concept with this comprehensive guide. Clean Design makes healthy beautiful and offers a plan for creating allergen-reduced home environments that protect families. For those who believe that your home is your sanctuary, this book is for you!"

—**Dr. Cheryl L. Dorsey, MD**
President, Echoing Green

"In a time where there is so much confusion about the toxins in our environment, particularly in our homes, Robin Wilson's work is necessary. She takes us along a journey examining simple steps each of us can take toward creating a healthier internal environment, which starts with where we live. As a mother and a wellness practitioner working with expectant and new moms, I highly recommend this book as an essential primer for anyone committed to wellness in their lives—one room at a time."

—**Latham Thomas, Maternity Lifestyle Expert**
Founder of MamaGlow.com
Author of *Mama Glow: A Hip Guide to Your Fabulous Abundant Pregnancy*

"Clean Design is a refreshingly simple approach to healthy living inside our homes. Readers are empowered with practical, hands-on suggestions and focused starting points for challenging areas in our living spaces. Robin Wilson continues to raise the bar by consciously creating and showing how to improve the quality of our lives."

—**Patricia Goodman, Artist**
www.patgoodman.net

"Happiness is pure, it's organic, clean, recycled, fashionable, and it's attainable. Robin Wilson helps us discover happier spaces by simply living a more conscious-lifestyle."

—**Nicole Friday**
Food & Lifestyle Blogger

Published by Greenleaf Book Group Press
Austin, Texas
www.gbgpress.com

Distributed by Greenleaf Book Group

For ordering information or special discounts for bulk purchases, please contact Greenleaf Book Group at PO Box 91869, Austin, TX 78709, 512.891.6100.

Design and composition by Greenleaf Book Group
Cover design by Greenleaf Book Group
Principal Photography by Vanessa Lenz and Matt Armendariz

Publisher's Cataloging Publication Data is available.

ISBN: 978-1-62634-189-0

Part of the Tree Neutral® program, which offsets the number of trees consumed in the production and printing of this book by taking proactive steps, such as planting trees in direct proportion to the number of trees used: www.treeneutral.com

TreeNeutral®

Printed in Canada on acid-free paper

15 16 17 18 19 20   10 9 8 7 6 5 4 3 2 1

First Edition

Other Edition(s):
eBook ISBN: 978-1-62634-190-6

CLEAN

WELLNESS FOR YOUR LIFESTYLE

DESIGN

ROBIN WILSON

WITH ALICE LESCH KELLY
PRINCIPAL PHOTOGRAPHY BY VANESSA LENZ AND MATT ARMENDARIZ

GREENLEAF
BOOK GROUP PRESS

This book is dedicated to my daughter, who reminds me why it is so important to share the simple ways to have a healthy and nontoxic living environment.

CONTENTS

FOREWORD

by Jordan S. Josephson, MD

It is an honor to write the foreword to Robin Wilson's *Clean Design: Wellness for Your Lifestyle*. This book provides sinus, allergy, and asthma sufferers with numerous options that can help with the management of their environment, leading to improved health, well-being, and quality of life.

Sinus sufferers with allergies and asthma tell me daily about how miserable they are because of nasal congestion, decreased sense of smell, debilitating sinus pressure, headaches, wheezing, sneezing, sniffling, snoring, and sleep apnea, and the many other troublesome respiratory symptoms they endure. I know exactly how they feel: Not only am I a physician who treats children and adults with these complaints, but also I am a fellow sufferer. I know what it's like to struggle taking a breath. I know how it feels to have allergies and sinus problems that cause debilitating post-nasal drip, cough, and hoarseness. But most importantly, I know how great you can feel when you apply the principles of Clean Design in your home as Robin Wilson describes in this phenomenal book. That's why I'm thrilled to recommend her *Clean Design: Wellness for Your Lifestyle* to individuals and families with sinus problems, allergies, and asthma.

Like me, Robin Wilson is an allergy and asthma sufferer who has built her professional life around helping others who are afflicted with respiratory disease. Robin's wealth of knowledge about Clean Design, and the ways in which environmental factors trigger asthma and allergy symptoms, makes her an incredibly unique health advocate and interior designer. Robin has the experience and expertise to help families create homes that truly are respiratory havens for people with allergies and asthma.

Within the pages of this book, Robin provides numerous ways to manage and eliminate allergy triggers in every room of your home, from the entryway and living areas to the kitchen, bath, and bedrooms. She even offers excellent tips on making outdoor living areas safer for family members and friends with allergies and asthma. Throughout this book, Robin shows readers how to use Clean Design guidelines to dramatically reduce exposure to dust, pet dander, pollen, mold, dust mites, smoke, household chemicals, airborne toxins, and other allergy and asthma triggers.

She also explains the importance of making eco-friendly design choices that contribute to the health of our planet as well as our loved ones.

And, to make sure readers know how beautiful Clean Design can be, Robin furnishes dozens of photos of living areas created according to her allergy- and asthma-friendly guidelines. Her gorgeous design photos are proof that you can eliminate and manage allergy and asthma triggers *without* compromising on style.

Minimizing allergens in the home is an essential way to protect the health and quality of life of people with allergies and asthma. One of the simplest ways to do this is to follow the Clean Design suggestions in this book. Doing so will help your precious children, beloved family members, and friends breathe easier in every room of your home.

—Jordan S. Josephson, MD
Board-Certified Otolaryngologist at the Manhattan Eye, Ear & Throat Hospital
Director, New York Nasal and Sinus Center
Clinical Assistant Professor, Hofstra Medical School
Founder, Sinus and Nasal International Foundation
Author of *Sinus Relief Now* (www.sinusreliefnow.com)
www.drjjny.com

ACKNOWLEDGMENTS

Thank you to those who have been a positive force in my life—from ensuring that the straight path did not create complacency to being there when a rocky path challenged my willpower and faith—so that the lessons I learned could be processed with clarity.

My parents have been unwavering in their support, especially recently—and I am so grateful to them as they ensure the path for both their granddaughter and me!

I especially thank the authors of two books who have inspired my continued quest to focus on this dream career, *The Alchemist* by Paulo Coelho and *The Dream Giver* by Bruce Wilkinson, which have many dog-eared pages.

Thank you to the friends who have remained close from the towns in which I have lived—Austin, Texas; Cambridge, Massachusetts; Manhattan, New York; Washington, DC; and West Orange and Montclair, New Jersey—and since I cannot name each of you, please know that your communication with me remains cherished and I am honored to be your friend.

This book would not be possible without travel to beautiful places, clients with elegant spaces, and the team of professionals (designers, interns, investors, attorneys, bookkeepers, photographers, videographers, tech guys, and more!) who have worked with me over the past years. And a special thanks to the licensing and retail partners who have supported the eco-friendly message . . . thank you all for believing in my vision to build a company focused on a well-oriented lifestyle.

Robin

INTRODUCTION

Everything You Need to Know

This is a book for all people who want to detoxify their home environment. Although my driving force has always been to create living spaces that protect people with allergies and asthma, my advice is appropriate for anyone who wants to live in a purer, less-toxic home. Whether you are building a new house or decorating your first apartment, whether you are setting up a nursery, furnishing a dorm room, or downsizing from a house to a condo, the information in this book will help you make smart, healthy design choices. Sometimes my suggestions will be dramatic—for example, if you have wall-to-wall carpeting that is older than eight years, I am going to advise you to remove it and install hardwood, tile, and throw rugs or carpet tiles—but most of my Clean Design recommendations will fit into your decorating budget. In fact, some of my best tips—such as replacing vinyl shower curtain liners with nylon liners—cost only a few dollars.

The book is organized by starting with a room-by-room breakdown of design options and a compendium of photos of the work from my firm, Robin Wilson Home—so that you can see the results of eco-friendly design that is also aesthetically beautiful. In the second section, I explain the elements of Clean Design, showing why it matters and giving the basics about your best choices for furniture, wall and floor coverings, window treatments, and cleaning tips. I will also channel my grandmother's and mother's "clean-machine" zeal and explain how best to clean your home. Each chapter will teach you how to implement Clean Design strategies for every room of your home, from "foundation to furnishings."

REAL STATISTICS

Sixty million Americans—that is one in five of us—have asthma and allergies.[1] We sneeze, sniffle, and itch. Expose us to a whiff of dust, a gust of pollen, a sniff of perfume, or an encounter with an inquisitive dog or cat, and before we know it, our airways start to close up, and we begin to cough, wheeze, or struggle to breathe.

Asthma and allergies cannot be cured, but they can be managed. We can reduce and prevent sneezing, wheezing, and other common allergy and asthma symptoms by avoiding the allergens that trigger them. Unfortunately, the average home is full of allergy and asthma triggers, which means that the place that should be your sanctuary can be a major source of wheezing and sneezing for those who suffer from respiratory issues. Leading triggers include

- Dust mites in beds and pillows
- Dander from pets
- Mold growth in walls, bathrooms, and basements
- Pollen from outdoor trees and grasses infiltrating your sleep space and living room sofa

- Fumes from cooking and chemical cleaners
- Toxic or environmentally unfriendly building materials that permeate indoor air

You can change all that. Using the Clean Design strategies in this book, you can create a healthy home environment that manages the indoor air quality and protects your family from the dust, mold, pollen, fumes, odors, airborne toxins, chemicals, and other substances that set off allergies and asthma. You can create a home environment that nurtures good health.

Although my focus in this book is on Clean Design, I will also share some of my favorite tips about eco-friendly design. Even a simple decision like selecting an energy-efficient appliance or lightbulb may not affect your health, but making eco-smart design choices contributes to the health of the earth—and ultimately, that helps us all.

HEALTHIER WAY TO LIVE

My Clean Design strategies are not only about better health. They are also about making your home look beautiful. A home decorated with Clean Design can be every bit as attractive as an allergy-triggering home. With Clean Design, every room of your home, from attic to basement, entryway to bedroom, can look sensational while protecting your family from allergy and asthma triggers.

Plagued by allergies and asthma since infancy, I have become an expert at Clean Design—creating allergen-reduced home

FOUR PRINCIPLES

Robin Wilson Home defines the four principles of eco-friendly design that we follow in all our projects as: sustainable, reusable, recyclable, and nontoxic. From the aesthetic beauty of organic and sustainable textiles to cork, bamboo, or hardwood flooring to low-to-no VOC paints, it is my belief that consumers are more excited than ever about the array of building materials available. Even a decade ago, there were few options in the marketplace, and today there are so many options, but with a twist, for example: wall insulation is now made of recycled blue jeans or newspapers; flooring may be reclaimed from old barns; and lighting may be passive prism or highly efficient fiber optic.

environments that protect families. Clean Design leads to amazing results: fewer allergy symptoms and asthma attacks, easier breathing, and better overall health. Having experienced these incredible results in my life, and with my toddler, it is thrilling to be able to share these tips and tricks with you. Clean Design is beautiful, as you will see from the first section of the book—*you will not have to give up style!*

Although Clean Design is perfect for people with allergies and asthma, it is not only for those of us whose bodies react to allergens and environmental toxins. The substances that cause "indoor air pollution" are a threat to everyone. According to the American Lung Association, "poor indoor air quality can cause or contribute to the development of infections, lung cancer . . . headaches, dry eyes, nasal congestion, nausea, and fatigue"[2] in anyone, not just those of us who suffer from asthma and allergies. We can *all* benefit from living in a purer home environment.

Clean Design is simple to implement. In the pages that follow, I will show you, step by step, how to use Clean Design to create a stylish, healthy environment in your home. Whether you live in a house or an apartment, a dorm room or a condo, you will be able to recognize the simple options so that your lifestyle will ensure a beautiful, comfortable, allergen-free space to come home to every day.

MY STORY

Clean Design is not only my passion—it is a way of life, given my history as a "pan-allergic" (defined as *allergic to everything*) child. When I was growing up, my parents were fortunate to find a pediatrician who recognized that my internal and external environment had to be changed. On many occasions my parents rushed me to the hospital; I experienced anaphylaxis due to ingesting dairy products;

breathing difficulties a moment after visiting the circus or riding a horse; and even the removal of my tonsils, which at the time was thought to be a therapeutic way to treat allergies.

Luckily, I grew up in Austin, Texas, a community in which organic food and alternative medicine were as common as cowboy hats and pickup trucks. My parents took me to countless doctors, and most of them prescribed regimens of powerful medications and steroids, but my parents were not convinced. Eventually my parents found a doctor whose holistic approach was ahead of his time. Giving my parents advice that changed my life, he recommended that they remove all possible asthma triggers and allergens from our home. His philosophy was "you can raise a sick child on strong medicine, or raise a strong child who is rarely sick." My doctor also created an organic diet and exercise program for me (swimming, track, bicycling, tennis) that would improve my health, strengthen my body, and help increase my lung capacity.

Following the doctor's holistic prescription, my parents devoted themselves to my health, tearing out wall-to-wall shag carpeting, installing hardwood and tile flooring, relocating our dog to the yard, removing curtains and installing blinds, washing my pillowcases weekly, keeping me away from allergy-causing foods, and feeding

me an organic diet. Based on the doctor's philosophy—"the home is the basic foundation for health"—my mother became a cleaning machine, working tirelessly to rid our living space of any traces of pollen, mold, dust, bacteria, animal dander, and other toxins that could harm me. My parents' commitment to Clean Design paid off, and within a few months of the changes, my asthma attacks became less frequent.

As a child, I was often trapped indoors, so I became an avid reader. My brother would go out and play, but I had to limit my time outside because pollen and other allergens would set off my asthma. Through my window I would watch other children playing while I stayed inside, my nose running, my lungs wheezing, my eyes itching, my stomach aching from allergic reactions to foods.

As I got older my health continued to improve. Early protection from a constant onslaught of environmental allergens, coupled with my strong exercise regimen and organic diet, strengthened me and allowed me to live a normal, successful life. This means that I still have to be careful to avoid allergens and triggers, but thanks to my parents' unwavering efforts, I grew up to be a resilient, healthy adult, who is not dependent on medicine on a daily, weekly, or monthly basis.

Today, as the mother of a toddler, and with many clients who seek out our Clean Design philosophy, my goal is to live in a home that is as allergen-free as possible, with a hope that it will help prevent my daughter from developing the allergies and asthma that plagued my childhood. *(We are blessed that she is fine thus far . . .)* And my lifestyle brand, Robin Wilson Home, is now sold at retail and allows many consumers to live a hypoallergenic lifestyle; all the products have been tested in my home or by my interior design clients in their living spaces, furniture, bedding, and cabinetry to ensure a wellness lifestyle.

My team shares a philosophy similar to the holistic doctor who treated me as a child. We are convinced there is a link between environmental toxins, indoor air quality, and allergies, asthma, and some other health problems. We believe the chemicals we are exposed to in our homes and offices have the power to make us sick, and we can improve our health and wellness using the Clean Design principles. We hope that you will enjoy reading about the options available to you and that you will learn how to use Clean Design to create a healthier living space for you and your family.

SECTION I

PORTRAITS OF CLEAN DESIGN:
IDEAS AND INSPIRATION

Chapter 1

ENTRYWAYS AND MUDROOMS

During a recent speaking engagement, an audience member asked me what the easiest thing is that someone can do to improve their space in one weekend if they are on a limited budget. My response: "It costs you nothing to take off your shoes when you enter your living space. By doing this you leave the toxins outside, rather than tracking in pesticides, bacteria, dirt, and pollen onto your floors or carpets."

The core principle of Clean Design is to limit external toxins, dirt, and chemicals in your home—and an entryway, foyer, front hall, or vestibule is the first and easiest place to implement your strategy. This gateway to your living area welcomes you, your family, and your guests into your home, and this space is the first line of defense to ensure that the space in which you live, eat, sleep, entertain, and relax is as nontoxic as possible.

Entryways come in all shapes and sizes. You may have a dramatic two-story entryway with storage areas, closets, a powder room, and a grand staircase. Or you might have a tiny space that is just big enough for opening the door. Whatever the dimension, its design must be inviting and stylish, setting the tone for the rest of your home. Its function must be versatile and useful, offering space for greetings and good-byes and a place to put the things we use to go from outside to inside and then back out again. Either way, your entryway has a lot of work to do. And in the homes of people concerned about allergies, asthma, and indoor air quality, the entryway provides a barrier, a place to leave behind the outdoor toxins and allergens that can pollute the rooms inside—a place where the elimination and management of allergy and asthma triggers begins.

The foyer or mudroom is the typical entry point for a home, and simple design, such as a built-in shoe cubby—or a haphazard array of shoes—will make most people feel that the home is "lived in" and will gain instant comfort points from a visitor. For others, installation of a bookcase wall or placement of a bench to allow shoe removal can be an efficient use of space.

Many homes have more than one entryway. You may access your home through a side door, backdoor, garage, porch, or mudroom. Wherever you and your guests come in, you can make it a stylish space that does everything you need it to do, welcoming people into your home and giving them a place to transition from outside to inside. Think about the foyer as a location for family and friends to deposit their coats, shoes, and boots. This is where they remove their coats, which can carry dust, pollen, cigarette smoke, perfumes, and other respiratory irritants. It is where they take off shoes and boots that have trudged on dirty sidewalks, muddy streets, and grassy areas frequented by dogs and other animals that relieve themselves in yards, on sidewalks, and in parks. Furniture options should include closets, cubbies, or a rack set aside if you are hosting an event. If there is no room for storage, coats and shoes should be removed at the door and carried to a closet elsewhere in the home.

COME ON IN

When you are designing and decorating an entryway, it may be helpful to think of it as a place where family members and guests can get rid of the dirt that they bring in from the outdoors.

After spending a day in New York City, I am especially anxious to take off my shoes because I think of pigeon droppings, animal waste, and walking through grungy subway or commuter rail stations. Whatever is in the puddles or stains on those walkways is definitely not something that should be brought much farther past the entry foyer in my home.

The best Clean Design option, which is often not possible, would have every entryway with a powder room on the side with a touchless faucet and toilet, where you could pause to handle your ablutions before entering the other rooms—allowing you to rinse away pollutants and germs picked up in the outside world. We all know that washing hands is one of the best ways to avoid spreading germs that cause illnesses, such as colds and flu, and other surface bacteria.

TAKING THE MUD OUT OF MUDROOMS

We don't call them "mudrooms" for nothing. Like all entryways, mudrooms can get dirty very fast, especially when there are kids in the house—family mudrooms have a tendency to fill up with everything from soil-encrusted soccer cleats to soaking wet snow pants. The best strategy with mudrooms is to make them as cleanable as possible by covering floors and walls with washable materials that can be easily scrubbed. Add wall hooks for wet clothing and cubbies for storage (and to keep junk off the floor), and remove anything damp so mold does not grow.

DESIGNING YOUR ENTRYWAY

As with all other rooms, your personal taste should determine what decorating choices you make. Overall, I suggest a fresh, streamlined look for entryways. Create a sense of peace, serenity, and welcome with calming wall colors and ample light from windows or light fixtures. Here's a simple checklist of features to include when possible:

- Install a light in the closet to help people find their coats, hats, umbrellas, shoes, etc.
- Hang a wall mirror as a nice focal point for the space.
- Limit clutter in the space by removing excess photos, pictures, and wall hangings.
- Select flooring that can handle wear and tear and is easy to clean. Hardwood is an excellent choice, as is tile and stone.
- If you opt for a carpet, area rugs, or a floor mat, select styles that can be easily cleaned.

When there is space, a table can be a helpful addition in an entryway, but select a surface that is easy to clean and that will not scratch easily from keys, purses, or other items. Try to be meticulous about the table being an "in-out area" so that excess papers will not accumulate, because it is an unwelcome sight for people entering your home and can also become a dust collection point. And finally, if there is room, a wood or leather chair or bench in your entryway allows people to sit when removing shoes or boots.

Chapter 2

LIVING ROOMS

*"I'm such a girl for the living room. I really like to stay in my nest and not
move. I travel in my mind, and that's a rigorous state of journeying for me.
My body isn't that interested in moving from place to place . . ."*

—bell hooks

I always find it interesting when entering large houses to
discover living rooms that are perfectly decorated—but
completely unlived in. So many people design their living
rooms for show, rather than living, and as a result, they
hardly ever venture into them. Maybe they gather in their
living rooms during parties or holidays, or when special
visitors drop by. But most days of the year, the living room
sits empty while everyone "lives" in other parts of the house.

Relaxed comfort is usually a top priority in living spaces
that are used daily—and it should be. Unfortunately, though,
the decorating style that is often associated with relaxed

comfort is the opposite of Clean Design, and it can be unfriendly to people with allergies and asthma: deep-cushioned sofas, fluffy pillows, cozy throws, shaggy wall-to-wall carpeting, coffee tables crowded with knickknacks, walls cluttered with framed photos, and piles of toys, games, books, electronics, and all the other items we enjoy using during our downtime. Do not worry: You will not have to give up comfort in order to have a living space that supports respiratory health. Using Clean Design, you can decorate your living space in a relaxed, comfortable way that eliminates and manages allergens and asthma triggers.

Whether you and your family spend most of your leisure time in the living room, the family room, or a "great room" that incorporates parts of several rooms, the spaces in which you live your everyday life are typically the most actively used part of your home. For design purposes, let's call this area your "living space" because it is where you and your family relax, watch television and movies, listen to music, play board games, read, and spend time with friends. Living spaces have to meet the needs of everyone in your family.

STANDARD DESIGN PROTOCOLS

Here are a few measurements that can help you as you design your living room:

- Distance from the coffee table to the sofa should be 18 inches.
- Distance between the sofa and end tables should be 3 inches on either side of sofa and table.
- Modern end tables should be 24 inches tall.
- Antique end tables are typically 27–29 inches tall.
- Upholstered sofas should be 36 inches deep (from seat cushion edge to outside back).

Clean Design Living Space Guideline #1
Beautify Your Fireplace without *Fire*

Gorgeous fireplaces often serve as a focal point in living areas. But using fireplaces to burn wood is not recommended for asthma sufferers and family members with allergies, because the smoke, allergens, and gases released by the flames can trigger asthma attacks and respiratory allergies. But do not worry—even without a roaring flame, fireplaces can still add style and drama to a room. Here are some tips for dressing up unused fireplaces:

- Choose a dramatic mantle, such as a gorgeous piece of stone, marble, or hand-crafted wood.
- Think carefully about your over-mantle décor. Consider a large mirror, photograph, or painting that sets the design tone for the room.
- Arrange birch logs with white bark on the fireplace grate.
- Create a still life inside the fireplace opening. Include pottery, vases, a small sculpture, or anything else you enjoy collecting. Talk with an electrician about the best way to light the space, either with a ceiling spotlight or tiny lights mounted inside the fireplace opening.
- Arrange plants of different heights in matching pots in front of the fireplace opening.
- Instead of a fireplace grate inside the fireplace, opt for multilevel candelabras with fragrance-free candles. (Candles bother some asthma sufferers even if they have no fragrance, so burn them only if they do not trigger wheezing and sneezing.)
- Place a beautiful screen in front of the fireplace opening—nobody will ever know that the fireplace is unused.

Clean Design Living Space Guideline #2
Clean Flooring Regularly

Whether a tile, hardwood, or carpeted floor, it is important to clean on a weekly basis, if not more frequently.

Clean Design Living Space Guideline #3
Toxic Foam Cushions Removal

A great movie to watch is called *Toxic Hot Seat* (Burbank, CA: HBO Documentary Films, 2013), and you will learn that most people die in fires from the toxic fumes emitted from cushions—and many of these cushions also off-gas, which impacts the air quality in your home. A great resource to educate yourself is the Sustainable Furnishings Council website, as they have a manufacturer certification program for those furniture makers who do not use toxic materials.

Clean Design Living Space Guideline #4
Limit Phantom Power

Living an eco-friendly lifestyle means managing power usage for the environment. Even people who try hard to use electricity wisely may not realize that "phantom power" usage

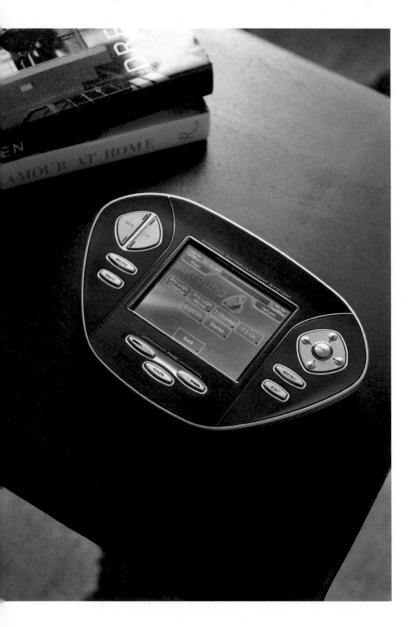

occurs anytime an item is plugged into an outlet. For example, did you know that even if your cell phone is not plugged into the charger, the charger is still drawing a small amount of electrical power from the outlet?

Televisions, computers, video recorders, electronic games, and many other items still draw power even if they are turned off. By being plugged in, they use up small amounts of power that add up over time. "The average U.S. household spends $100 per year to power devices while they are off (or in standby mode),"[3] according to the U.S. Environmental Protection Agency on the Energy Star website. "On a national basis, phantom usage accounts for more than 100 billion kilowatt hours of annual U.S. electricity consumption and more than $10 billion in annual energy costs."[4] Here are a few steps to limit phantom power usage in your home:

- Unplug chargers when they are not in use.
- Use a power strip as a master switch and turn it to the off position so that certain products do not stay on all the time, such as game stations and stereos. Use one for home electronics and another for your computer and all peripheral equipment.
- Consider a TV that turns off completely and eliminates power usage or an Energy Star–certified product, which will be among the lowest phantom power users in its category.
- Enable the sleep settings on your computer and monitor, so they go into power save mode when not in use.

Chapter 3

KITCHENS:
HEARTH OF THE HOME

I always laugh when I look around at my home during parties. Friends and family are supposed to be in the living areas, but where do I find them all? In the kitchen, of course. As the song by Paul McCartney and Wings goes: "No matter where I serve my guests, they seem to like the kitchen best . . ."

In most homes, the kitchen is the center of action—the "hearth of the home." I think of it as the nexus point for family interaction and entertainment. It is where families gather to share meals, catch up on the day's news, and hang out. In homes or lofts with open floor plans, kitchens merge with living areas, becoming a place to watch television, catch up on email, play, and do work as well as to prepare and consume food.

However, for those with allergies and asthma, the kitchen can be a source of triggers with fumes, cleaning solutions, and food allergens. But Clean Design can help you with your

STANDARD DESIGN PROTOCOLS

Here are a few measurements that can help you as you design your dining space:

- Height of a modern dining table should be 28–30 inches tall.
- Standard chairs are typically 18 inches tall and 18 inches wide.
- The apron (underside) of table should not be lower than 26 inches, for lap clearance of a diner.
- Passage area around table is usually 36 inches.

design specifications for certain materials, and help you with the management of allergens and asthma triggers so that your kitchen can be welcoming to all your family members and guests.

QUESTIONS TO ASK DURING THE DESIGN PROCESS

If you are lucky enough to be starting from scratch, you have many decisions to make, and everything should be selected based on how you live, relax, and entertain. Will your kitchen be one large space or several smaller spaces? If you have a larger space, you may opt to have two or three interconnected areas, such as a breakfast nook for casual meals or snacks, a food preparation and cooking area, a pantry, and a living area where family and friends can gather and relax. An island is another gathering spot where meals can be served buffet style, and barstools invite casual interaction. However, if you have a metropolitan apartment, your space options might be limited, so it is key to make strategic storage and material decisions based on your needs and budget.

Even if you are not launching a major redesign, there are many changes you can make that will benefit the environment and your family's health, from countertop options that are antibacterial and less porous, to microwaves and countertop appliances that cook efficiently with infrared technology to limit exposure to fumes.

In the pages that follow we discuss the top Clean Design Kitchen Guidelines, which are crucial for your smart kitchen.

Clean Design Kitchen Guideline #1
Make Room for Recycling

Gone are the days when all we needed was one waste container. Now, our commitment to the environment calls on us to separate glass, plastic, and paper from our kitchen waste stream. Having space in the kitchen or pantry for individual bins—a recycling center of sorts—makes it easy for every family member to help keep trash out of landfills.

Clean Design Kitchen Guideline #2
Choose Eco-Friendly Cabinetry

When you choose kitchen cabinetry, be sure that it is made with low-VOC (volatile organic compound) paints, stains, and adhesives, and that there is no formaldehyde in the adhesives. These features are important in all home furnishings, but they are especially crucial in the kitchen, where temperatures are raised and lowered during the cooking process several times a day. Changes in temperature cause off-gassing of toxins, and no room (other than the bathroom) has as many temperature variations as the kitchen. I like "frameless" or European-style kitchen cabinets. Frameless construction uses 10 percent less wood and is great for allergy and asthma sufferers because interiors are more accessible for cleaning than framed cabinets. Typically, the European-style cabinets are used in perimeter cabinets, with framed cabinets used on island installations.

Cabinetry: Holiday Kitchens; Contractor: Kingdon Knowles

THE RWH LINE OF CABINETRY FROM HOLIDAY KITCHENS

My favorite cabinetry manufacturer is Holiday Kitchens (www.holidaykitchens.com). In fact, I like the company so much that I have licensed my brand, Robin Wilson Home, to their RWH line of eco-friendly kitchen cabinetry. There is so much to like about Holiday Kitchens because it is made in the USA since 1946, in a Wisconsin factory that employs over 250 people.

Each RWH custom cabinet incorporates resource-saving European-style, frameless construction; uses nontoxic adhesives, paints, and stains; and provides clients with over one hundred door styles and endless finish options, so each kitchen is uniquely custom designed for the consumer, with a short, six- to eight-week factory turnaround. And the cabinetry has a lifetime warranty because the team makes a durable product, not a disposable product! Plus, I love the fact that Holiday Kitchens is a sustainable manufacturer—they plant two trees for every one used, resulting in over 24,000 trees planted in the past few years.

Holiday Kitchens is a pioneer in the eco-friendly home design movement, with the majority of its cabinetry made from sustainably forested wood that is computer cut and used in a way that minimizes waste. Leftover wood is utilized in many ways: Wood chunks are fashioned into cutting boards, shavings become animal bedding, and sawdust is sold for use as fire-starter pellets. The company keeps its costs manageable by working with small, independent dealers who are strong community citizens in their towns.

Holiday Kitchens, one of the nation's top custom kitchen cabinet manufacturers, is leading the way to create an affordable, functional, and environmentally friendly product. And with so many options in the RWH line, clients can be happy if they have a modern or a traditional design aesthetic.

Clean Design Kitchen Guideline #3
Provide Ample Ventilation

Smoke and other allergenic substances are released into the air during cooking, so it is important to have a strong exhaust fan that vents outdoors. One of the brands with a narrow profile and low noise options is BEST, which has options that can be vented externally, the most effective way to clean air quickly. I also recommend cracking open windows when you turn on the oven to allow air to circulate.

Clean Design Kitchen Guideline #4
Store Food with Care

Store all food in sealed containers and all food waste in BPA-free containers with lids to control pest issues. If family members or frequent visitors have food allergies, store allergenic foods in a separate area, carefully sealed and labeled to prevent accidental consumption and cross-contamination.

Clean Design Kitchen Guideline #5
Choose Under-Cabinet Lighting Wisely

Low-profile under-cabinet lighting provides atmosphere and a good light source for food prep. Options include xenon, LED, or fluorescent lights. (I do not recommend using low-voltage halogen bulbs because they have a short lifespan and generate heat.) LED lightbulbs last longest, do not heat up, and can be easily installed with new low-profile bars or flexible strips. Xenon lights have the most natural light and can be dimmed using standard ballasts. Fluorescent lights are the least expensive, but their light can be harsh and feel like an aquarium. For safety and energy efficiency, my suggestion is use of LED lights for under-cabinet visibility. (Learn more in chapter 14.)

Clean Design Kitchen Guideline #6
Choose Countertops That Keep Their Clean

There are many options for countertops, including composites, concrete, granite, PaperStone, wood, soapstone, marble, and bamboo. Stainless steel is commercial, modern looking, and nearly indestructible, although it does show fingerprints. The list is practically endless.

If you like granite or other kinds of stone countertops, be sure to follow the manufacturer's guidelines about sealing it regularly. The same is true of cement. If you do not, the stone or cement has natural fissures, which can absorb meat juices and other liquids, and bacteria can multiply in an unsafe way.

A unique, eco-friendly product is a surface called PaperStone. Believe it or not, it really is made from paper—it is 100 percent post-consumer recycled paper held together with cashew-nut resin. You know it is tough, because it was originally designed for skateboard ramps. It has multiple color options, and it is warmer to the touch than stone. PaperStone is stain- and heat-resistant, FSC-certified, and aesthetically beautiful, although it does have a tendency to fade with long-term exposure to natural sunlight.

Nonporous solid countertops, such as Silestone or quartz, are antibacterial, easy-to-clean, and durable. The firm Cosentino offers choices in Silestone (www.silestoneusa.com) and other great products such as Dekton (www.dekton.com) or ECO (www.ecobycosentino.com), which is groundbreaking for the materials used to manufacture it: crushed glass, mirrors, recycled porcelain from sinks, and fly ash from smokestacks, all held together with a corn resin polymer. All options are quite durable and come in a variety of colors.

Clean Design Kitchen Guideline #7
Fight Bacteria
You may notice that some of the suggestions in this book relate to bacteria—for example, I like countertop materials that do not harbor harmful bacteria. Although bacteria may not trigger allergies and asthma, people with respiratory illnesses sometimes have compromised immune systems. This means that if they do come in contact with harmful bacteria or other germs, such as viruses that cause cold and

flu, their chances of getting sick can be higher because their immune systems may not be able to do as good a job fighting off the bacteria. My recommendation is a nonporous solid quartz countertop. See chapter 11.

Clean Design Kitchen Guideline #8
Select a Smart Sink
Did you know that the edge of a drop-in sink can be a breeding ground for bacteria, salmonella, and mold? Because of this, I recommend "undermount" kitchen sinks for all homes, but especially for homes with allergy and asthma sufferers. With an undermount sink, the lip of the sink is mounted below the countertop. This means the sink sits beneath the countertop rather than on top of it. Another benefit of an undermount sink is that it is easy to wipe food scraps and crumbs from the counter to the sink—there is no exposed edge to get in the way. And some quartz products offer a solid countertop with a built-in sink that gives you the lip-free effect of an undermount sink.

Be sure to use water-efficient faucets, which use far less water than old-fashioned water-wasting models. Look for products bearing the EPA's WaterSense label,[5] which is similar to the Energy Star program for appliances and indicates that the faucets have aerators to make water droplets feel bigger and other technologies to improve the flow of water.

Clean Design Kitchen Guideline #9
Choose Energy-Smart Appliances

Appliances have two costs: the price paid for purchase, and bills paid for energy usage. When choosing new appliances, look at their price tags and their bright-yellow Energy Guide labels, which explain energy usage costs. Always look for the Energy Star logo, because this rating can save significant costs over the life of the appliance. This certification program was designed for consumers in a partnership with manufacturers and the U.S. Environmental Protection Agency to improve energy efficiency, cut energy bills, and help protect the environment by reducing the emission of greenhouse gases. Energy Star–certified appliances use 10 to 50 percent less water and electricity than standard models. Ignore any salesperson who says you can get ALL rated appliances, because *stoves are not rated.*

DO'S AND DON'TS FOR KITCHEN REMODELING

Remodeling a kitchen is a huge, expensive job, and we recognize that working with a Certified Kitchen Designer (CKD) is a first step. And definitely consider an independent kitchen dealer over a big-box retailer; you will be surprised by the options and value. Here are some value conscious do's and don'ts to consider before you start:

- **DON'T remodel your kitchen for a prospective buyer,** because you may not get back 100 percent of what you spend. Typical payback is 50 to 80 percent, with the less personal, mass-market renovations (example: neutral colors/white cabinets) receiving the most payback.

- **DO create a list of "absolutes" before you walk into a kitchen design meeting.** If you are not sure beforehand what you want and do not want, you are likely to be seduced into buying unneeded items.

- **DO think about colors and styles before you walk onto a sales floor.** Read design magazines and tear out photos in advance, or the sales rep may convince you that there is a certain bestseller that is really a higher-priced choice—it could be the model the salesperson is trying to unload, or he or she is getting a "special promotion" from the manufacturer.

- **DON'T design your kitchen with someone else's life in mind.** If you cook frequently and have a busy kitchen full of people, then avoid countertop materials that scratch and stain easily or that need regular maintenance. Likewise, if you hardly ever cook, do you really need a six-burner stove and restaurant-quality range?

- **DON'T buy a "faux-pro" model or Professional Series** because most mainstream appliances (ranges/refrigerators) perform just as well.

- **DON'T choose a range by BTU alone.** An extreme BTU number does not guarantee better performance. It is less expensive to find a range with at least one high-BTU burner that you can use if you need high heat quickly.

- **DO go by more than price when choosing a contractor.** Ask to see a recently installed kitchen, visit an online reference service (like Angie's List), and ask to see a kitchen that was installed three years ago to see how it has stood the test of time. Be sure to receive a copy of the contractor's license and insurance information.

- **DON'T opt for extended appliance warranties.**

- **DO expect delays.** Ask your contractor for a completion date, but plan for at least two extra weeks to ensure final details.

- **DON'T buy a built-in refrigerator** ($3,000+) when you can buy a cabinet-depth refrigerator for less and often find more options.

Clean Design Kitchen Guideline #10
Save Energy with Refrigerators and Dishwashers
The refrigerator and the dishwasher are the biggest energy users in your kitchen. You can save energy and money with kitchen appliances by using the following energy-saving tips, provided by Energy Star (www.EnergyStar.gov):

Dishwashers[6]

- **Scrape, do not rinse.** Rinsing dishes can use gallons of water before the dishes are even loaded. Save yourself the rinsing—just scrape food off dishes. *Consumer Reports* is a great resource to use to understand which dishwashers and detergents are designed to maximize cleaning so you do not have to prewash. If your dirty dishes sit overnight, use your dishwasher's rinse feature. It uses a fraction of the water needed to hand rinse.
- **Load it up.** Dishwashers use about the same amount of energy and water regardless of the number of dishes inside, so run full loads whenever possible, or consider a dish drawer model so you can wash a partial load with less water.
- **Skip the heat.** Select the no-heat drying option because most models provide good drying results without the extra energy usage.

Refrigerators[7]

- **Set the appropriate temperature.** Keep your refrigerator at 35 to 38 degrees Fahrenheit.
- **Place your refrigerator in a cool place.** Position your refrigerator away from a heat source such as an oven, a dishwasher, or direct sunlight from a window.
- **Allow air circulation behind the refrigerator.** Leave a few inches between the wall and the refrigerator, and keep the condenser coils clean if you have an older model. Read the user's manual to learn how to safely clean coils. Coil cleaning brushes can be purchased at most hardware stores.
- **Check the door seals.** Make sure the refrigerator seals around the door are airtight. If not, replace them. And if your refrigerator is older than ten years, consider replacing it because it is probably less efficient than modern units.
- **Keep the door closed.** Minimize the amount of time the refrigerator door is open.

APPLIANCE BUYING GUIDELINES

Robin Wilson Home has worked on a few projects that were required to exceed minimum standards of energy efficiency. We have a checklist of a few items you might want to consider:

- **Washer/Dryer:** Our favorite brands use 40 percent less energy when the Eco-Normal cycle is selected. Sensors are in place to allow clothes to dry more efficiently, and water usage is minimal in the washer—you could save over $800 (estimated) in energy usage during the first five years of use. We always recommend top-load washers *without the agitator,* as they use less water and do not have mold retention issues like some front-load washers.

- **Dishwasher:** There are hundreds on the market, and the best models for energy efficiency have a light and a normal cycle that allow flexibility for water usage. For those with smaller dish loads, we recommend dish drawers.

- **Refrigerator/Freezer:** More families are opting for separate units if they have the kitchen space, which means that the freezer stays closed most of the time,

given that the refrigerator is opened more frequently during daily food preparation. Also, many people have a separate beverage/snack refrigerator (door or drawer style) that allows the refrigerator to remain closed much of the day. To prevent mold growth, be sure the units have drainage pans that are easy to clean.

- **Air conditioners:** In-wall air units are never as efficient as central air systems. However, if you do have an in-wall unit, please make sure to install a Plexiglas or permanent surround so that there is limited air seepage in/out of your home.

- **Countertop appliances:** Place all the items on a master switch (except microwaves and coffee makers) and/ or unplug all the units that are not in use to prevent "phantom power usage," especially those appliances with power digital clocks or timers.

Chapter 4

BEDROOMS: ONE-THIRD OF YOUR LIFE

*Do you know the answer? Ask the average consumer when they last washed or replaced their pillow, and the typical honest answer is **six years ago!***

We spend one-third of our lives sleeping, and yet studies have found that bedrooms can be the dirtiest and most allergenic rooms in many homes. That is because sheets and bedding are not washed often enough, allowing a tremendous buildup of dust mites, pet hair, mold, and other allergens. What is more, people often decorate bedrooms in a way that makes them difficult to clean. It is no surprise, then, that more than one-third of the people polled in a recent study said that they suffer more allergy symptoms in their bedrooms than in any other room in their homes.

If your bedroom is causing you to sneeze and wheeze, it is time to make some changes using my Clean Design principles,

eliminating allergens and managing asthma triggers.

Because we spend so many hours sleeping in our bedrooms, it is best to try to make them the cleanest rooms in our homes. By following our ten Clean Design guidelines for a bedroom, you can create stylish, cozy bedrooms that are clean, healthy, and beautiful. The overall message with bedrooms is to keep them clear and clean. The less clutter you have in a bedroom, the less opportunity for dust collection. Go for a simple, sophisticated design that is easy to keep clean and free of allergens.

MATTRESSES: RESTING EASY

You spend a third of your life sleeping, so it makes sense to choose a mattress that supports your health and your sleep. I recommend mattresses made with sustainable, natural materials such as cotton and natural latex rather than synthetic foams that off-gas into your bedroom air. Buying an eco-friendly mattress that does not spew toxins into the air is the first step in managing your Clean Design efforts. Like sofa cushions, mattresses and pillows are a breeding ground for dust mites. You can protect yourself from these allergy- and asthma-triggering bugs by encasing your mattresses and pillows in washable, allergen-proof, dust mite–proof covers.

Clean Design Bedroom Guideline #1
Manage Floor Dust

Floors collect more dust than any other surface in a room, and carpets and rugs hold on to that dust, no matter how frequently you vacuum. The best solution for bedroom flooring is to skip the carpeting and rugs completely; however, that is typically unrealistic, so a simple alternative is to use an area rug that does not completely cover the floor, or to use a rug on either side of the bed so that it can be regularly cleaned and you can clean underneath the bed. Hardwood floors feel best on your feet, although some clients in southern climates have used ceramic tiles that resemble wood. Or you may opt to select FLOR carpet tiles (www.flor.com), which are washable and can be removed easily if you decide to make changes back to the original hardwood or tile flooring.

Clean Design Bedroom Guideline #2
Break the Budget on Your Mattresses

The cheaper the mattress, the more chemicals inside—and if you think about the fact that your face lies next to the mattress for many long hours every night, it is worth it to spend a bit more to get the best quality mattress you can afford. Not only do cheaper mattresses contain flame-retardant chemicals, which are a hazard for allergies, but also some synthetic mattresses are made with petroleum-based fibers that contain chemicals such as antimony (arsenic), boric acid (roach killer), deca (flame retardant), and formaldehyde, a known

carcinogen often used as an adhesive.[8] They can also cause cancer with prolonged exposure.[9] The best choices are latex, eco-foam, or other nontoxic, chemical-free, hypoallergenic mattresses with strong back support that ensure a good night's sleep.

The least toxic mattresses are made with sustainable, natural materials such as cotton and natural latex. Often, people will purchase a synthetic foam mattress and end up returning it because it will off-gas for several months, and some people find that the smell will disrupt their sleep and cause respiratory issues.

When buying mattresses, sofas, or any home furnishing containing foam, always ask

your retailer directly if furniture contains flame retardants or if the product is made with formaldehyde-based fire retardants. Two good resources are The Clean Bedroom retail chain (www.thecleanbedroom.com) and the Sustainable Furnishings Council (www.sustainablefurnishings.org).

Clean Design Bedroom Guideline #3
Hypoallergenic Pillows Are a Must

Hypoallergenic pillows are a must—because people with allergies and asthma often experience respiratory issues during the night, which is due to lower cortisol levels at night, a reaction to dust mites, and/or a reaction to the dander in a down feather pillow. Pillows are a breeding ground for dust mites, the microscopic bugs that live in all homes and feed on the flakes of skin that slough off the bodies of humans and other living things. You cannot be fully rid of dust mites, but you can take steps to greatly reduce their numbers in your home.

A good hypoallergenic pillow setup will have three layers: the pillow, a zippered pillow cover, and the pillowcase. Avoid down pillows and blankets, because they can trigger allergy and asthma symptoms and are typically dry clean only, which can add to the toxins in your sleep space. Make sure you follow the rule of threes: Wash zippered cover every three weeks, wash pillow every three months, and replace pillow every three years. Here's a great tip: Consider taking old pillows to an animal shelter where they can be used to cushion wire cage floors.

Clean Design Bedroom Guideline #4
Use Hypoallergenic Covers for Mattresses

Mattress pads allow you to utilize the protection of a cover that can be washed, and to extend the life of the mattress. Imagine not having a mattress pad, and the dust mites keep building up in the actual mattress—which would mean that only one year after purchase, the mattress will weigh more than when you bought it. Because many people keep a mattress for up to ten years, that would mean your bedroom could become a "wheezing and sneezing" chamber and not a relaxing sanctuary. You can protect yourself from these allergy- and asthma-triggering bugs by encasing your mattresses and pillows in washable, allergen-proof, dust mite–proof covers. After you cover your mattress with a cotton hypoallergenic cover, you should wash the cover every two to three months at minimum.

Clean Design Bedroom Guideline #5
Choose Fabrics You Can Live (Well) With

Buy the best sheets you can afford, and make it a priority to select hypoallergenic bedding, even if it costs a bit more—because your health is priceless. Remember that bedding textile fabrics are next to your skin and face for hours at a time, and any toxins they release will be absorbed quickly in the sleep state. In bedrooms, it is more important than in any other room in the house to use eco-friendly, allergy-friendly bedding and fabrics. The best options are cotton, silk, corn fiber, bamboo fiber, and soy fiber made without formaldehyde. Cotton is soft and durable, a perfect fabric for bedding materials. To manage dust mites and other allergens, wash sheets, pillowcases, and blankets in water heated to at least 130 degrees Fahrenheit on a weekly basis.

Clean Design Bedroom Guideline #6
Decorate with Useful Furniture

A blanket chest or foot bench at the end of the bed made from sustainably forested wood is a great place to store extra blankets, pillows, or keepsakes; plus it will give you a perfect spot to get dressed in the morning. My other recommendation is to have a side table with a drawer for storage space and enough space solely for a lamp, book, and bottle of water so you do not clutter your sleep space. If you have the space, it is nice to have a seating area with comfortable chairs, chaises, or other furniture, which will allow for relaxing or reading.

Avoid bargain-basement or discount furniture, because it is likely to contain formaldehyde adhesives that will off-gas into the room and create a toxic load that could affect your health. Buy from vendors that use eco-friendly and sustainable practices for harvesting their wood, and who use nontoxic glues and low- to no-VOC paints and stains. (For more on selecting eco-friendly furniture, see chapter 12 "Furniture and Furnishings.")

Clean Design Bedroom Guideline #7
Simple Window Treatments

"Dust collectors" is a good phrase to use for heavy draperies or curtains that are cleaned infrequently. For a modern space, consider side panel curtains made of linen or cotton, offset by mechanized window shades that are recessed into a soffit for a completely clean look. A more traditional space might look better with shutters, blinds, or pull-down shades made of natural materials. Overall, the key is simplicity and ease of washing.

Clean Design Bedroom Guideline #8
Keep Allergens off Walls

Clean Design means you recognize that the largest surface in any space is the walls. It is a great idea to use low- to no-VOC paint in all rooms, and

Q: HOW MUCH SLEEP DO WE REALLY NEED?

A: The basic answer to this question is that you need enough sleep to be able to function well during the day. Exactly how many hours this is varies based on age and differences among individuals. Here are the recommended guidelines from the Centers for Disease Control for nightly sleep:[10]

- Preschoolers: 11–12 hours
- School-aged children: At least 10 hours
- Teens: 9–10 hours
- Adults: 7–8 hours

especially important in bedrooms. First, the paint is a bit thicker than a standard paint, which means you only need one coat. Second, the paint typically has a built-in primer so you have less labor when painting. And finally, one hour after painting, there is no paint smell because the paint self-seals to limit release of toxins into the air. The typical paint job requires weeks of airing out a room, and even then it continues to release toxins into the air, causing these allergy- and asthma-triggering fumes to be inhaled for extended periods of time.

Another option is wallpaper, but be sure to select options that are not vinyl, and use adhesives that are safe and environmentally friendly, which will typically not trigger

asthma and allergy symptoms. (For more details, see chapter 11 "Surfaces.")

Clean Design Bedroom Guideline #9
Avoid Closet and Surface Clutter

Pollen, mold, dust, and other allergens settle on knickknacks and other items. Sure, you can clean them, but it is much easier when bedroom surfaces are relatively clear of stuff. To keep dust buildup to a minimum, keep belongings in covered boxes, bins, drawers, cabinets, and bookcases with doors. Better yet, store them outside of the bedroom. Not only do they collect dust, but also books—especially older ones—can be a source for growth of mold spores.

And do not forget your closets! Keep them as clutter-free as possible—closets tend to be

dust mite havens because of all the clothing and junk that sits in them and collects dust. Clean closets twice a year by removing everything, cleaning thoroughly, mopping or steam cleaning the floor, and putting back only what you really need. If your closet has carpeting, I recommend ripping the carpet out, and installing tile, Marmoleum, or hardwood. Donate or recycle clothes, shoes, purses, and other items you do not use or wear. Keep clothing that is not worn frequently in zippered bags, and shoes in non-paper boxes.

Clean Design Bedroom Guideline #10
Don't Let Bedbugs Bite

Bedbugs thrive in mattresses, and people with allergies and asthma need to be cautious to avoid them, because bites can cause allergic reactions, skin rashes, and other symptoms. The most likely place to run into bedbugs is in hotels, although it is also possible for guests to bring them into your home.

Frequent travelers are at most risk of being affected by bedbugs; even fancy hotels can have them. The trick is to check the bed for signs of bedbugs before settling into your room. Here's how to avoid them at a hotel: When you check into a room, leave your luggage in the entry foyer hall when you first enter your room. Do not bring your luggage fully into a hotel room until you check for bedbugs, because they can hitch a ride home with you on suitcases, duffel bags, and clothing. Go to the mattress, lift up the head of the mattress, and look for little pinpoint-sized bloodstains between the mattress and the box spring. Also, inspect the mattress and box spring for dead bedbugs. If you see blood or bug remains, the bed probably has bedbugs. Ask for a new room, or switch hotels. To find out if bedbugs have been reported in a hotel you are considering, check out the Bed Bug Registry (www.bedbugregistry.com), a free public database of bedbug sightings in the United States and Canada.

But more important, the key is to prevent

infestations at your home if you should encounter them. When you return home, wash everything immediately and do not store your luggage in your bedroom closet—if necessary, keep luggage in the garage, patio/deck, or a storage space for a week. Since bedbugs are parasites that feed on blood, they love to spend time in warm, humid places near humans. If you deprive them of their food sources, then they may not survive to migrate to your bed.

TIPS FOR BETTER SLEEP

Reducing the allergen levels in bedrooms can make a huge improvement in the quality of your sleep—it is hard to get a good night's sleep when you are wheezing and sneezing! Beyond that, there are several other steps you can take to get better sleep. Check out tips from the National Sleep Foundation[11] and the Mayo Clinic.[12] Here is a summary of some of the best tips:

- **Keep a regular schedule.** Go to sleep and wake up at about the same time each day.
- **Avoid napping.** Daytime naps—especially late in the day—can interfere with nighttime slumber.
- **Snack small.** Eating a large meal before bed can keep you awake. If you must snack before bed, eat something that is not fatty or spicy and contains no caffeine. Consider something like fruit, half a turkey sandwich on whole-wheat bread, or unsalted popcorn.
- **Limit caffeine.** Individual caffeine tolerance varies, and if you are particularly sensitive to its effects you may have to dispense with coffee, tea, cola, and other caffeinated foods as early as mid-afternoon.
- **Beware of alcohol nightcaps.** Although alcohol may make you sleepy at first, it can have the opposite effect later in the night. Nicotine may also interfere with sleep.
- **Create a bedtime routine.** Meditate, listen to calming music, read books, or take a warm bath before turning in.
- **Remove distractions.** Rid your bedroom of electronics, work materials, and anything else that is not associated with peaceful slumber.
- **See the light.** Exposure to natural light during the day helps your internal clock stay on schedule.
- **Move your body.** Exercise helps improve your ability to sleep. Some people find that if they are active too close to bedtime, it keeps them awake; others find a brisk walk shortly before bed helps put them right to sleep. Figure out what works best for you.
- **Get help.** If you struggle to sleep, see your health-care provider—do not try to treat it on your own with over-the-counter sleep aids and supplements that make dramatic promises. Millions of Americans suffer from some kind of sleep disorder. Your health-care provider can diagnose and treat insomnia, sleep apnea, and other sleep problems.

Chapter 5

BABY NURSERY

A wise woman once said: You do not get a do-over on a child, so you must treat everything and every moment as special. And keep the nursery as a safe and peaceful room in your home, no matter what . . .

Our babies are the most precious family members, and using Clean Design protocols to design and decorate your baby nursery will allow you to make smarter choices about what your newborn is exposed to as he or she begins to grow and build immunity. Our immune systems protect us from harmful bacteria, viruses, and other threats—but, when babies are born, it takes six to twelve months for their immune systems to mature. Thus, until their immunity is stronger, it is best to limit contact with toxins or allergens that can trigger the body into a reactive state.

Using Clean Design will assist you as you eliminate and manage asthma triggers and germs, and allow you to make

good choices about furnishings—from furniture and paint to toys and bedding. You can also take steps to keep allergens out of your baby's environment by keeping the nursery—and the rest of the house—as free as possible of toxins such as cleansers, fumes, and other substances that can begin a cycle of wheezing and sneezing for susceptible children.

There is a school of thought that children are *less* likely to develop reactions when exposed to allergens early in life. Others say that you should keep a laboratory-clean room environment. But scientists and pediatricians are divided, and while the researchers sort it all out, we stand firmly committed to the idea that during those early months of life—especially until the first birthday—all babies should be protected from allergens, toxins, and hormone disruptors. More studies are needed to get to the bottom of the issue, but the important thing to remember is that babies must have time for their immune systems to develop and strengthen.

A typical newborn sleeps fourteen hours or more per day, which means that the mattress, furniture, flooring, paint, and linens in their sleeping area should be as nontoxic as possible. And the air should be as clean and allergen-free as possible. With more parents co-sleeping with their babies, either in the bed or in a bassinet on the side of the parents' bed, it is also important to ensure that the mattress, pillows, and linens in the master bedroom remain hypoallergenic.

Designing for a baby's arrival and the nursery is a bit like designing any other bedroom, but the stakes are higher. As a new mom, my baby came home to a nursery that was completed two months prior to her arrival so any fumes could off-gas, and her room was designed with all the Clean Design guidelines you will see on the next few pages. We will show you how to eliminate and manage allergens and asthma triggers in your nursery and create an eco-friendly design and sleeping haven for your little one.

Clean Design Nursery Guideline #1
Choose Eco-Friendly, Baby-Safe Furniture

It is easier to find toxin-free children's furniture now because as parents make it a priority, more manufacturers are adding eco-friendly baby furniture to their product lines. Be sure to shop with a reputable retailer who works with eco-friendly furniture manufacturers. All furniture—cribs, chests of drawers, nursing rockers, changing tables, and other furniture in your nursery—should be free of formaldehyde adhesives and manufactured with low- to no-VOC paints and stains.

One of your purchases is likely to be a rocker

or glider. These chairs are a cozy, convenient place to cuddle and feed your baby. Choose one that has a removable slipcover and ensure that it is not pretreated with stain removers, because your baby will often rest his or her head on the fabric when you are cradling them during nursing.

Most people do not think about the crib, but during teething months, most babies begin to chew on the side rails of the crib, so you want to be sure that the paints or stains are nontoxic. And since babies roll on the floor, crawl, and are close to the ground, your flooring is another key component of safe design. Know what is next to your baby's skin and ensure that you see our Resource Guide at www.cleandesignbook.com for more suggestions.

Clean Design Nursery Guideline #2
Select a Super-Safe Mattress

Clean Design principles are most important when it comes to your baby's crib mattress. In my opinion, buying a nontoxic crib mattress is the single most important purchase you can make for your baby's health. Crib mattresses can be a major source of chemicals in a baby's environment, and based upon multiple studies, when brand-new, most conventional mattresses off-gas because they are manufactured with polyurethane foam and polyester foam padding, which are loaded with chemicals. Some companies will advertise their mattresses as soy, cotton, or other material, but the outer cover defeats everything if it is vinyl.

I was shocked recently when I read about a University of Texas at Austin study done in 2014 by a team of environmental engineers, in which researchers identified more than thirty chemicals in the crib mattresses they analyzed, including phenol, neodecanoic acid, and linalool. "The most abundant chemicals identified in the crib mattress foam, such as limonene (a chemical that gives products a lemon scent), are routinely found in many cleaning and consumer products."[13] The researchers said they conducted their study because infants are considered highly susceptible to the adverse health effects of exposure to indoor air pollutants. The University of Texas environmental engineers discovered other chilling information as well: "VOC levels were significantly higher in a sleeping infant's breathing zone when compared with bulk room air, which means an infant sleeping on a new crib mattress is exposed to about twice the VOC levels as people standing in the same room."[14]

Additionally, "because infants inhale significantly higher air volume per body weight than adults and sleep a longer time, they experience about 10 times as much inhalation exposure as adults when exposed to the same level of VOCs," the researchers said.[15] If that information does not make you buy eco-friendly, nothing will!

Crib mattresses are at their worst when they are brand new. The University of Texas study found that "new crib mattresses released about four times as many VOCs as older crib mattresses."[16] Older crib mattresses,

which have had time to off-gas and air out, release lower levels of VOCs than new mattresses. However, older mattresses may contain other harmful chemicals such as flame retardants that are now banned in mattress foams.

Because of research like this, I feel 100 percent sure that babies should have new, organic, eco-friendly, toxin-free mattresses. Yes, they cost more than discount crib mattresses, but ask yourself: Would you want your baby to breathe fumes from a chemical factory? See our Resource Guide at www.cleandesignbook.com for shopping suggestions.

Clean Design Nursery Guideline #3
Protect against Dust Mites

Dust mites are a major cause of allergy and asthma symptoms. Research suggests that reducing contact with allergens such as dust mites may delay or prevent a baby or child from developing allergy or asthma symptoms, according to the American Academy of Allergy, Asthma & Immunology.[17] You can minimize dust mites in your nursery by encasing your crib mattress in zippered, "allergen-impermeable" hypoallergenic covers. Do not bother with bumpers, blankets, or pillows. Not only do they collect dust, but early in a baby's life, they pose a suffocation, strangulation, and entrapment danger as well. Once a week, wash crib bedding in hot water.

Babies should not sleep with stuffed toys, because they raise the same risks as bumpers. But often a security toy is used to soothe older babies to sleep, so you must also wash them regularly to rid them of dust mites. Wash the stuffed animal at least once a month inside a pillowcase to limit wear and tear. However some cannot be washed, so another option is to place it in the freezer inside a zippered plastic bag for twenty-four hours. The freezing process will kill any mites, and you can simply shake the bag before

taking the stuffed animal out so that the dust mite carcasses fall to the bottom of the bag.

Clean Design Nursery Guideline #4
Choose Nontoxic Products for Walls, Floors, and Windows

As recommended for other areas in your home, I suggest painting the nursery with low- to no-VOC products. Paint the room several months before baby's anticipated arrival, and ventilate well while painting. Expectant moms should ask someone else to paint the nursery while they are away from the home; not only should you avoid fumes, but as your center of balance changes during pregnancy, you are at a higher risk of falling off ladders or step-stools.

For floors, I recommend hardwood finished with low-VOC stains long before baby settles in. Avoid wall-to-wall carpets, which trap dirt and allergens. To soften the floor, opt for washable area rugs or FLOR carpet tiles that can be cleaned regularly. If you have wall-to-wall carpeting that cannot be removed, have it professionally steam cleaned without any added chemicals four times a year.

For nursery windows, stay away from dry-clean-only curtains that collect dust. Select easy-to-wash cotton or linen fabric, wood blinds, or shades, and vacuum or wipe up dust with a damp cloth once a week.

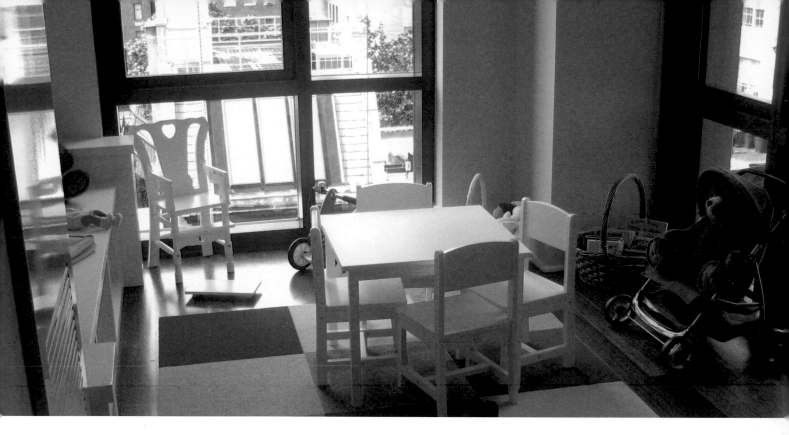

Clean Design Nursery Guideline #5
Keep the Room Super Clean

No matter how hard you try, allergens will still make their way
into the nursery. You can get rid of them by cleaning carefully.
It does not have to take long—rooms that are created using
Clean Design can usually be cleaned quickly.

Vacuum floors at least once a week using a vacuum with a
HEPA filter—and my favorite is the Panasonic JetForce vacuum
series, designed to ensure that the self-contained centrifuge
and washable filters prevent dust from getting blown back into
the air while you vacuum. Hardwood floors can be mopped
or vacuumed as well—and we recommend using a clean
mop dampened with water or all-natural, toxin-free soap or
cleanser.

All nursery visitors should take their shoes off at the front
door, to ensure that the entire home has floors that remain relatively clean. While you are cleaning, wipe dust off furniture,
walls, doorframes, ceilings, and air vents.

Clean Design Nursery Guideline #6
Ensure Good Ventilation

If you would like to add additional ventilation and air cleaning to your nursery, you can use a stand-alone air filter. Not all experts agree on the helpfulness of these machines, but some think they are a good idea. You can also improve ventilation in the nursery and throughout your home by changing your heating and air-conditioning filters more often than their manufacturers recommend, and by using HEPA filters in all ventilation devices.

On days when pollen is not high, crack open the windows in the nursery to let air flow through for fifteen minutes. Remember, though, that no matter how well ventilated your home is, you should never allow anyone to smoke, because secondhand smoke contains chemicals that can harm babies and cause asthma.[18]

Clean Design Nursery Guideline #7
Keep Humidifiers Clean

Some pediatricians suggest running a cool-mist humidifier in the nursery when a baby has a cold or congestion. If your doctor recommends one, remember it's crucial to keep them clean. I recommend cleaning humidifiers daily. Use white vinegar and a clean toothbrush to scrub out any areas that look dirty or moldy. Then rinse well with hot water. The manufacturer may recommend using bleach for cleaning, but since some may remain on the surfaces, I do not like the idea of bleach being vaporized into nursery air and breathed by your baby. Overall, use humidifiers only if your baby's health-care provider recommends them, because they can raise humidity in a room enough to encourage the growth of mold, which is a potent allergy and asthma trigger.

FEEDING YOUR BABY FOR ALLERGY PREVENTION

How you choose to feed your baby is obviously not a design decision, but it does have an impact on your baby's health. I'm not a doctor, but I am a new mommy. And I have read many books and worked with a doula, pediatrician, baby nurse, and caregiver who have all devoted their lifetimes to raising healthy children.

My pediatrician recommended that breastfeeding be done for my child as long as possible, given my genetic history with allergies and asthma. After successfully breastfeeding for sixteen months, we have a healthy baby who has experienced no respiratory issues (so far!), thus I am convinced that breastfeeding is a smart choice for all babies, if at all possible. And it is especially smart for those babies with a suspected genetic predisposition to respiratory issues such as allergies and asthma. Studies have shown that breastfeeding may help lower the chances of allergies developing in babies, and in those studies, babies who were exclusively breastfed for at least four months "had a lower risk of milk allergy, atopic dermatitis (commonly known as eczema), and wheezing early in life."[19]

Researchers do not know for sure why breastfeeding offers allergy protection, but they believe one reason is that breast milk contains substances that strengthen a baby's immune system. Another possibility is that breast milk contains "friendly" bacteria (like that found in yogurt and other fermented foods) that help support the baby's digestive health and build immunity. Babies who are breastfed receive many other health benefits as well. Whether or not there are allergies or asthma in a family, lowering allergy risk is one of many reasons to breastfeed.

According to the American Academy of Pediatrics, breastfeeding provides a protective effect against respiratory illnesses, ear infections, gastrointestinal diseases, and allergies, including asthma and eczema. The rate of sudden infant death syndrome (SIDS) is reduced by over a third in breastfed babies, and there is a 15 to 30 percent reduction in adolescent and adult obesity in breastfed versus non-breastfed infants. The American Association of Pediatrics recommends "exclusive breastfeeding for about [the baby's first] 6 months, followed by continued breastfeeding as complementary foods are introduced, with continuation of breastfeeding for 1 year or longer as mutually desired by mother and baby."[20]

Chapter 6

BATHROOMS

We have several friends who were trying to get pregnant. We told them to remove the vinyl shower curtain liner and replace it with a nylon liner. And a few months later . . . baby on the way. Remember: We highly recommend against using vinyl, which contains phthalate chemicals that are believed to be hormone disruptors.

Bathrooms are smaller than most other rooms in the house but have the potential to be the biggest trouble spot—from the humidity that can lead to mold growth, to the spray from a toilet flush that can expose family members to bacteria, and to the off-gassing from toxic cleansers or vinyl shower curtains—creating a brewing chemical stew to cause an *unfriendly* environment for the health of a home's inhabitants. Using Clean Design principles will eliminate and manage allergy and asthma triggers in every bathroom, which is important because of all the water-oriented tasks performed here. Even if your family takes brief showers, bathrooms tend toward dampness because of teeth brushing,

face washing, and toileting. You can design a space and select accessories to ensure aesthetic beauty and focus on a healthy environment in your home.

Clean Design Bathroom Guideline #1

Watch Out for Mold

Mold is every bathroom's nemesis, and managing the places with a humid environment should be your focus—shower curtains, shower enclosures, and leaky faucets or toilets. Humidity enables the growth of mold, which is a major allergy and asthma trigger. Implement a few simple steps to help manage bathroom humidity:

- **Take shorter showers.** Showers account for approximately "17 percent of residential indoor water use,"[21] according to the Environmental Protection Agency. That adds up to nearly 40 gallons of water per day for the average family, and 1.2 trillion gallons of water per year in the United States![22]

- **Use water-efficient faucets and showerheads.** Old-fashioned showerheads can spray out as much as 4 or 5 gallons of water a minute, while a water-efficient showerhead uses no more than 2 gallons of water per minute; look for products bearing the EPA's WaterSense label, which is an EPA-certified program similar to the Energy Star program for appliances. Switching to a WaterSense-certified showerhead can save an average of 2,900 gallons of water per year.[23] All products bearing the WaterSense label must be independently certified to ensure they meet EPA water efficiency and performance criteria. If you do not like the feel of water-efficient showers, choose one with an aerator that makes the water droplets feel bigger.

- **Turn off the water while you brush.** We have all done it—we let the water run while we stand there brushing our teeth. Save water, money, and humidity by turning off the tap for the five minutes it takes to brush.

- **Install an exhaust fan.** Be sure that it vents out of the house and that it is running whenever someone is taking a shower or bath. If you do not have an exhaust fan and installing one is not feasible, open the window for five minutes until the humidity has left the room.

- **Fix leaky faucets and toilets.** In addition to being an incredibly huge waste of water, a simple drip from a faucet or toilet can create a perfect environment for mold growth.

- **Wipe up condensation and any other moisture.** If dampness gathers on bathroom windows, walls, floors, or other surfaces, wipe down daily. Use a squeegee on glass shower doors and tile.

- **Use mold-resistant paints.** Bathroom paint is a specific type that repels mold and mildew growth, and it is different from the standard wall paint. Select this specific option and be sure to choose low- to no-VOC formulations so they do not off-gas into the space.

- **Avoid wallpaper in bathrooms.** Moisture can become trapped behind wallpaper in bathrooms—and it is not a pretty sight to see the walls after wallpaper removal, with black mold growth on drywall surfaces. Choose paint for bathroom walls.

Q: WHAT IS A STEAM SHOWER, AND SHOULD I CONSIDER INSTALLING ONE?

A: Steam showers have been used in homes for decades. They continue to be popular with designers, architects, and homeowners because they are water efficient. Families who have a child or elderly person with skin conditions, asthma, or allergies can benefit from the use of a therapeutic steam shower; the steam can help improve breathing and reduce muscle tightness during an asthma or allergy attack. My favorite brand is Mr. Steam, which uses a minimal amount of water with fewer components to ensure durability.

Panasonic WhisperGreen Select Bathroom Fan

A NEW SHOWER CURTAIN, THEN A BABY

When I first moved into my former husband's apartment, he had a vinyl shower curtain liner. We had been trying to get pregnant for about three months, but I was so busy doing the move, redecorating the rest of the apartment, and researching to find our new suburban home. One day, I realized it was time to focus on the bathroom. The first item on the list was replacing his vinyl liner with a nylon shower liner. We conceived within a month, and while I have no proof that changing the shower curtain liner helped, I can tell you this fact—some vinyl shower curtain liners are made with bisphenol-A, or BPA. BPA is an endocrine disruptor, which means it can interfere with human reproduction. I am just saying . . .

Clean Design Bathroom Guideline #2
Use Only Nylon Shower Curtain Liners
One of the best clean-air tips is also one of the cheapest: replacing your vinyl shower curtain liner with a nylon liner for less than $20. What is wrong with vinyl shower curtains or liners? Plenty. Made with a material called polyvinyl chloride (PVC), vinyl shower curtain liners hold on to mold spores, encouraging mold growth. What is worse is that vinyl shower curtain liners release harmful toxins into your home's air. That "new shower curtain" smell in vinyl is caused by high concentrations of chemicals that are linked to serious health problems, according to researchers at the Center for Health, Environment & Justice (CHEJ). Results from a CHEJ study found that shower curtain liners made with PVC plastic contain many harmful substances, including VOCs, phthalates, and organotins. These chemicals can lead to adverse health effects, including respiratory irritation; central nervous system, liver, and kidney damage; nausea; headaches; and loss of coordination.

Amazingly, CHEJ found that PVC shower curtains released 108 different VOCs into the air. Here's what CHEJ Science Director Stephen Lester said when the study was released: "The release of so many volatile organic compounds, many of which are toxic, raises serious questions about the risks PVC shower curtains pose to families, especially young children exposed to these vapors. Every effort should be made to eliminate PVC shower curtains from homes and to replace them with safer alternatives."[24]

Nylon shower curtain liners, on the other hand, do not off-gas chemicals, do not hold mold the way vinyl does, and can easily be washed in the washing machine.

Glass shower doors are an even better idea, because they are the easiest surface to clean, and they can be recycled years later when the bathroom is renovated.

Clean Design Bathroom Guideline #3
Choose Natural Fabrics

Like vinyl, many synthetic fabrics and rugs disperse toxins into the air. To avoid this, use environmentally friendly cotton textile—for towels, rugs, curtains, visible shower curtains (not the liners), and robes. Other options include linen, silk, or bamboo. However, you should know that bamboo fiber is really a rayon-type material after the strands are broken down from the original grass stage.

Clean Design Bathroom Guideline #4
Install High-Efficiency Toilets

According to the EPA, "Toilets are by far the main source of annual water use in the home, accounting for nearly 30 percent

of an average home's indoor water consumption!"[25] So, it makes sense to install high-efficiency toilets. Older toilets use as much as 6 gallons per flush; new high-efficiency models use as little as 1.28 gallons or less per flush.[26] (Dual-flush toilets, which use less water for liquid waste than for solid waste, are also a good option.) Lower water bills will repay you for whatever you spend buying and installing a new toilet.

No matter what type of toilet you have, keep this important tip in mind: Always lower the toilet seat when flushing to ensure that spraying particles do not land on or near towels, toothbrushes, and soaps. If you have an opportunity to fully renovate a bathroom, try to design a water-closet space that separates the toilet from the rest of the room.

WASH YOUR HANDS LIKE A PRO

You have been washing your hands since you were a toddler—but do you really know how to do it right? According to the Centers for Disease Control, follow these steps for washing your hands and share them with your children, who are often the germ carriers from school to the home:[27]

- **Wet** your hands with clean, running water (warm or cold), and apply soap.
- **Lather** your hands by rubbing them together with the soap. Focus on the back of your hands, between your fingers, under your rings, and under your nails.
- **Scrub** your hands for at least twenty seconds— about the time it takes to hum the "Happy Birthday" song twice from beginning to end.
- **Rinse** your hands well under clean, running water.
- **Dry** your hands using a clean towel, or air dry them.

Clean Design Bathroom Guideline #5
Select Eco-Friendly Cabinetry

Bathroom cabinets should be as environmentally friendly as any other furniture in your house. Choose cabinetry that is made with sustainably grown wood, formaldehyde-free adhesives, and low- to no-VOC paints and stains. Moisture can collect inside bathroom storage areas, so be sure to keep cabinetry, medicine chests, drawers, and other storage areas dry and clean. If you are building a new home or remodeling an older home, consider having the linen closet open into the hallway rather than the bathroom, because this helps keep prevent mold from growing on linen closet walls, shelves, and contents.

Clean Design Bathroom Guideline #6
Consider Tile, Quartz, or Stone for Floors and Walls

Tile and stone release few VOCs after installation and curing of grout—and these surfaces can be sealed, which reduces the chance of mold and mildew growth and ensures ease of cleaning. With proper maintenance, tile and stone will last more than fifty years. There are many eco-friendly tile and stone options available for bathrooms, so be sure to speak to your design professional and visit a showroom that has a variety of options for you to examine for look, feel, and layout.

Quartz surfaces have also been engineered with thin surfaces so they can also be used as wall cladding, countertops, and flooring with slabs that are typically delivered in 8 foot × 4 foot dimensions, to allow an almost seamless installation.

Clean Design Bathroom Guideline #7
Remember the Lights!
Bathroom lighting requires more thought than most people think—a single ceiling fixture or one above the mirror will create shadows. Lighting in layers is the best solution: mirror, shower, water closet, and tub area. It is also nice to place dimmers on the lights if you like to turn your bath into a spa experience. The perfect level for a wall sconce on either side of the mirror is 66 inches from the finished floor to limit shadows while shaving or applying makeup.

Chapter 7

HOME OFFICES

"Choose a job you love, and you will never have to work a day in your life."

—Confucius

Home offices can be a big source of toxins, dust, allergens, and asthma triggers, and most are more than ready for a major overhaul guided by the principles of Clean Design. Offices tend to fill up with files, magazines, books, reports, and other dust-collecting items.

Office equipment and electronics attract dust, and no matter how often you clean, it can be tough to keep office surfaces free of dust. Some equipment and supplies in offices release toxins into the air, and if ventilation is poor, we breathe air contaminated by these fumes. All of these factors can trigger allergy and asthma symptoms in susceptible people. Poor air quality also can bother otherwise

healthy people, causing irritation of the eyes, nose, and throat, as well as coughing, sneezing, and other symptoms.

As with every other room in your home, however, you can take steps that will make your home office's air healthier for you and your family and better for the overall environment. The best place to start is with my Clean Design Home Office Guidelines.

Clean Design Home Office Guideline #1
Decorate with Clean Design in Mind
Paint home office walls with low- to no-VOC paint, select toxin-free furniture, and minimize use of dust-collecting carpeting and window treatments, as you would in any other room in your home.

Clean Design Home Office Guideline #2
Minimize Clutter
The more "stuff" you have in your office, the more dust, allergens, and asthma triggers there will be. I know it is hard to de-clutter an office, but give it your best try. What you cannot get rid of can go in closed cabinets, drawers, and covered bins. However, schedule an annual review-the-files week to remove/shred old documents that are unnecessary.

Clean Design Home Office Guideline #3
Use Less Paper

Having a paper-free office is a great goal, but let's face it: Sometimes you need to print something. That is fine, as long as you try to use as little paper as possible. Think twice before printing, and when you do print, choose printer settings that allow you to print double-sided pages or multiple pages on one sheet of paper. When you buy paper, choose recycled paper or paper certified by the Forest Stewardship Council (www.fsc.org).

Clean Design Home Office Guideline #4
Buy Smart Equipment

Whenever possible, buy office equipment, computers, and supplies that are eco-friendly, energy-efficient, and toxin-free. Look for Energy Star–certified products, which use less energy than comparative items. For example, my Hewlett-Packard scanner turns off automatically after two hours if it has not been used.

Clean Design Home Office Guideline #5
Avoid Ozone

Ozone is a colorless gas that can damage our lungs. When we breathe in elevated amounts of ozone, it can cause coughing, wheezing, congestion, and even chest pain in anyone, but especially in people with asthma, allergies, and lung diseases such as emphysema and chronic obstructive pulmonary disease (COPD).

Although ozone occurs naturally in our atmosphere, it is also produced by some kinds of equipment and machinery. In home offices, ozone can be released into the air by some kinds of laser printers and copiers. You can avoid ozone by choosing products such as ozone-free laser printers. If that is not an option, make sure to use such ozone-creating equipment in large, well-ventilated rooms. In your home office, consider keeping a window open, running an exhaust fan, or using your home's air-conditioning system to keep air flowing well.

STANDARD DESIGN PROTOCOLS

Here are some general height and depth guidelines to consider when designing your home:

- Doorknobs 36 inches from floor to center of knob
- Counters 36 inches tall
- Bar 42 inches tall
- Bookcases 12–15 inches deep
- Desk 24 inches deep by 29 inches tall, at minimum

Clean Design Home Office Guideline #6
Watch for VOCs

These potentially toxic chemicals can be found in office equipment and supplies such as copiers and printers, correction fluids, carbonless copy paper, permanent markers, and graphics and craft materials such as glues and adhesives. Whenever possible, be sure to ventilate the area well while using them, or use a freestanding air filter in your home office.

Clean Design Home Office Guideline #7
Keep It Clean

Clean your home office thoroughly once a week, and remember to remove dust from easily forgotten places, such as behind cabinets, on top of bookshelves, under desks, around computer equipment, and on piles of books and papers. Keep in mind that computer keyboards and phone handsets can become laden with crumbs, bacteria, and sticky gunk from constant use. Clean them often according to their manufacturers' instructions.

Clean Design Home Office Guideline #8
Recycle

Always recycle paper, cardboard, plastic, and any other materials that can get a second life. Also, recycle electronic waste (old printers, phones, and computers), batteries, and compact fluorescent lights. Check with product manufacturers and your municipality's waste disposal office for details about how to recycle these items safely and effectively.

Clean Design Home Office Guideline #9

Catch Power Vampires

Wasting electricity is not a health issue, but it is a problem for the environment, and keeping power use as low as possible benefits us all. Even people who try hard to use electricity wisely may not realize that there are some surprising ways to save power. As mentioned earlier, even if your cell phone is not plugged in to the charger, the charger is still drawing electrical power from the outlet. This is referred to as "phantom power," and the products that use phantom power are referred to as "power vampires." (Read our tips in chapter 2 for Energy Star suggestions on using less phantom power in your home.)

Chapter 8

LAUNDRY ROOMS, BASEMENTS, GARAGES, AND ATTICS

*Some people have nontraditional relationships with domestic household chores—
it's not so unusual to meet a man who does most of the cooking, dishes, and
laundry, while a woman does the child care, recycling, or lawn work . . .*

Some of the most easily forgotten areas of the house—the laundry room, basement, and attic—can be big contributors to allergens, asthma triggers, and toxins in a home. Although these spaces are easy to forget, I hope you will bring your focus to them and make them an important part of your Clean Design strategy. With some simple changes in these areas, you can eliminate and manage allergy and asthma symptoms and go a long way toward creating a healthier home for everyone in your family.

THE LAUNDRY ROOM

The laundry space is one of the most utilized areas—and

usually one of the smallest rooms in a home—if you are fortunate enough to have a laundry room or closet. In most homes, the washer and dryer are relegated to a corner of the basement, the garage, or stuffed into a minuscule closet. And yet, the laundry area uses a big chunk of your home's water and energy. It is also the place where highly allergenic, potentially toxic washing and cleaning products are often stored and used.

Let's start with water. The average washing machine uses 41 gallons of water per load.[28] That is shocking when you realize that the typical family does 400 loads[29] of laundry per year—which means a significant use of water and electricity. You can save on utilities by purchasing a high-efficiency washing machine. These machines use 35 to 50 percent less water and 50 percent less energy[30] than standard low-efficiency models. Plus, they require less detergent, which can be environmentally friendly. Be sure to look for the Energy Star label when you shop for a washing machine, and remember that this certification does not apply to clothes dryers because there is little difference in energy use among models.

The U.S. Environmental Protection Agency runs the Energy Star certification, and you should always review the bright yellow labels when you are shopping for a new appliance because each tag offers info about energy usage by that product. The website for Energy Star has information about saving energy and eco-friendly "best practices." Here is a list of really helpful washer/dryer tips:

Clothes Washer Tips[31]

- **Use high-efficiency (HE) detergent in front-loading clothes washers.** Using regular detergent creates too many suds, which affects the machine's washing and rinsing performance. Over time, it can lead to odors and mechanical problems.
- **Run full loads whenever possible.** Clothes washers use about the same amount of energy regardless of the size of the load.
- **Wash in cold water.** Water heating consumes about 90 percent of the energy it takes to operate a clothes washer. Unless you are dealing with oily stains or white goods, washing in cold water will generally get the job done. An exception to this rule is bedding and any items that are breeding grounds for dust mites. Switching your temperature setting from hot to warm can cut energy use in half.
- **Avoid the sanitary cycle.** This super-hot cycle, available on some models, increases energy use significantly and should be used only when absolutely necessary.
- **Air-dry clothing.** Where and when possible, air-drying clothes, instead of using a dryer, not only saves energy but also helps them last longer. Hanging clothing on an internal rack is best if someone in your home is allergic to pollen, because hanging clothes outside can be an asthma trigger. Many people have a drying rack used regularly in the laundry area or the basement.
- **Activate the high-speed spin option.** If your clothes washer has spin options, choose a high-speed spin or

the extended-spin option to reduce the amount of remaining moisture in your clothes after washing. This decreases the amount of time it takes to dry your clothes.

- **Leave the front-load door open after use.** Front-loading washers use airtight seals to prevent water from leaking while the machine is in use. When the machine is not in use, this seal can trap moisture in the machine and lead to mold. Leave the door ajar for an hour or two after use to allow moisture to evaporate. Make sure children do not climb into the machine while the door is open.
- **Rinse the washer every month.** Some manufacturers recommend rinsing the washer

each month by running a normal cycle with 1 cup of bleach to help reduce the risk of mold or mildew buildup. Consult the product manual to review recommendations.

Clothes Dryer Tips[32]

- **Use the moisture sensor option if you have one to reduce energy use in your dryer.** Many new clothes dryers come designed with a moisture sensor, which automatically shuts off the machine when clothes are dry. Not only will this save energy, but it will also save wear and tear on your clothes caused by overdrying.
- **Clean the dryer's lint filter after every load.** Removing excess lint will improve air

circulation and increase the dryer's efficiency. It is also an important safety measure, because lint buildup can cause fires.

- **Scrub the lint filter regularly if you use dryer sheets.** Dryer sheets can leave a film on the filter that reduces airflow and, over time, can affect the performance of the motor. (My recommendation is that you do not use dryer sheets, since they typically contain perfumes and other chemicals that can bother people with allergies and asthma.)

Choosing Laundry Detergents

Laundry detergents can be a source of allergens and toxins, but there are steps you can take to make eco-friendly, health-supporting choices:

- Select concentrated high-efficiency (HE) detergent and follow the directions on your laundry detergent's box (and your washer's user's guide) regarding how much detergent needed in each load. Most consumers use too much, so follow the directions. Look for detergents low in phosphorus, which is an environmental pollutant that encourages the overgrowth of algae in waterways. Avoid perfumes and dyes, which can cause irritation for people with allergies and asthma.
- Labeling rules do not require complete disclosure of some kinds of ingredients. Contact laundry detergent manufacturer websites, tell them you are looking to avoid allergens, and ask for a detailed list of what is in their products. Talk with your health-care provider or allergist about what

allergenic ingredients you should avoid. Once you know what to look out for, do not rely only on the package's ingredient label.
- Choose nontoxic brands such as Seventh Generation, Caldrea, Method, or Mrs. Meyer's—but remember that because they are environmentally friendly does not necessarily mean they will not trigger allergies or asthma.
- For specific recommendations on environmentally friendly laundry products, check out Environmental Working Group (EWG) consumer guides. The EWG is an environmental health research and advocacy organization whose mission is to conduct research and provide information about protecting human health and the environment.

THE BASEMENT

Mold is the biggest basement concern for people with allergies and asthma, and since many basements tend to be damp, it is exactly what mold and mildew need to thrive. The Environmental Protection Agency recommends that homeowners avoid finishing a basement that is below ground level unless all water leaks are sealed first.

It can be difficult to deal with mold in finished basements, because wallboard, carpeting, and other design elements can cover the walls and floors where mold can grow. We recommend using paperless drywall in basements because the mold will not have a source to thrive. To prevent condensation, basements should have ample ventilation (heat and air conditioning, and an exhaust fan if/when needed), or you can also reduce moisture in the basement by running a dehumidifier. To prevent mold from growing in the dehumidifier's water collection bin, clean it regularly using a scrub brush, vinegar, and hot water.

Once mold and mildew start to grow in a home, it can be quite hard to get rid of the problem, so the best strategy is to try to prevent mold and mildew growth *before* it begins using several steps.

First, start by making sure there are no leaks in your basement, and check regularly for leaks and drips from pipes, water heaters, washing machines, sinks, and other water sources in your basement. If you discover a leak, dry the area completely and repair the source of the water as soon as possible.

Second, if any area in your basement gets wet—whether the cause is a leaky pipe or a big storm—be sure to dry all surfaces thoroughly within 24 to 48 hours. When you discover mold or mildew growing in your basement, remove or treat the affected area immediately. Mold and mildew take hold quickly, and removing water is the best defense against a "bloom" of mold in your home. If carpets, wallboard, or flooring are wet and cannot be dried, remove and dispose of them. Use products designed for mold removal or hire an expert to do it for you. Be sure to ventilate well during mold removal and follow the directions on the package of any products you use.

Finally, relocate any family members with allergies and asthma while a mold/mildew eradication project is under way.

THE GARAGE

Garages often serve as storage areas for an array of potentially toxic cleaning supplies, paints, hazardous materials, and pesticides. I highly recommend you get rid of as many of these items as possible, and store what you cannot dispose of in an outdoor shed, rather than an attached garage of your home. Even containers that seem to be tightly sealed can leak fumes that mix with household air, lowering your indoor air quality and contributing toxins, allergens, and asthma triggers to your family's home environment.

For the safety and health of your family, dispose of whatever stored chemicals you can do without. When you dispose of toxic products, be sure to do so safely. Contact your municipality for advice on how best to rid your home of these chemical troublemakers.

THE ATTIC

If you have an attic, do not just think of it as a storage area. The attic and roof provide many opportunities for energy savings. Provided you have no leaks, mold is not usually an issue in attics. But if water comes in, mold can grow, so make sure to check your attic for leaks several times a year and after big storms. If water leaks in, dry it promptly and have the leak repaired as soon as possible.

Do not use mothballs because they contain the chemical pesticides naphthalene or para-dichlorobenzene,[33] which can cause burning of the skin and respiratory tract and trigger asthmatic symptoms. To prevent moth infestation, wash clothes in the warmest possible water before storing. Place them in a cedar chest or pack them with cedar chips, cedar blocks, or other cedar products. The smell of cedar repels moths.

Most important, remember to clean your attic regularly and keep clutter to a minimum to prevent dust from gathering. Try to vacuum and dust your attic at least every three years! Adding proper insulation can reduce energy use (and costs). When adding insulation, be sure to work with a qualified contractor. Visit the U.S. Energy Department's website for more info about insulating your home.

Chapter 9

OUTDOOR LIVING

"People do not want to go to the dump to have a picnic, as they want to go out to a beautiful place and enjoy their day. And so I think our job is to try to take the environment, take what the good Lord has given us, and expand on it or enhance it, without destroying it."

—Jack Nicklaus

Clean Design goes beyond the four walls of your house and to the exterior—to your deck and yard. Certainly you have less control over the air quality outdoors than indoors—there are some days when allergy and asthma sufferers are simply better off staying inside with the windows closed and the air-conditioning on, either because of high pollen levels or heavy smog. But on days when outdoor air quality is good, friends and family with allergies can relax outdoors knowing that you've designed your outdoor living space to minimize wheezing and sneezing.

Here are my Clean Design Guidelines for creating an outdoor living space for your family and friends.

Clean Design Outdoor Living Guideline #1
Use Nontoxic, Eco-Friendly Building Supplies

The last thing you want in your outdoor living space is toxin-treated building materials. Decks, gazebos, picnic tables, and other outdoor structures should be built with sustainable, eco-friendly, toxin-free building wood or other materials. Avoid using composite or pressure-treated wood that is treated with chemicals—such as creosote, arsenic, or pentachlorophenol—and if you do have these materials in your deck or yard, manage risk by sealing them regularly according to safety guidelines and to avoid sawdust exposure.

The same is true of children's play structures—in the past, they were routinely constructed with composite wood products treated with toxic stains and varnishes, which is not a good idea at all. If you have children, be sure any play structures you have in your yard are made with safe, non-toxic, eco-friendly materials. Consider replacing a structure with recycled plastic products or wood that is coated with a low- to no-VOC stain.

Stone patios are an excellent eco-friendly alternative to decks. Aesthetically beautiful, durable, and naturally eco-friendly, they set the tone for relaxed, stylish yards.

Clean Design Outdoor Living Guideline #2
Pay Attention to Pollen

Pollen is worse at certain times—spring and fall, for example, and on warm, dry, breezy summer days. Pollen counts vary based on geographic location as well. You can find out how the pollen and mold levels are in your area by consulting the American Academy of Allergy, Asthma & Immunology's National Allergy Bureau map. Another great resource for people with pollen allergies is Pollen. com, which allows users to sign up to receive allergy alerts via email.

Keep in mind that your car is an outdoor living space that invites pollen exposure. You can keep pollen levels in cars lower by cleaning the car's interior often—weekly or even daily during the worst part of pollen season—and by driving with the windows closed and air-conditioning on. Set your car's air conditioner to take in fresh air unless you are driving behind an exhaust-spewing vehicle; when that happens, switch the air intake to "recirculate."

SKIN-SAFE SUNSCREEN

Some sunscreen ingredients cause skin reactions in people with dermatological allergies. Try PABA-free, fragrance-free, oil-free sunscreens, which are less likely to cause skin rashes.

Clean Design Outdoor Living Guideline #3
Plant with Allergies and Asthma in Mind
It's impossible to remove pollen from your yard. But you can take steps to manage pollen exposure by making landscaping choices that are less likely to contribute to wheezing and sneezing among your family members and friends. Before planting bushes, grasses, or trees, consider what types of plants your loved ones are most allergic to by reviewing a list of pollen sources that are particularly problematic, such as grasses and cedar and birch trees. By choosing plants that are not on the allergen list you reduce the chances of exposure to tree pollen, which is tricky, because wind can disperse it for miles. But even so, if you know your loved one is allergic

to oak, for example, it will certainly help to not have a giant oak towering over your yard.

Here is some great advice about landscaping and gardening with allergies and asthma in mind, provided by the experts at the Asthma and Allergy Foundation of America (AAFA):

"If you have asthma or allergies, you don't have to limit your yard decorating to stones and concrete! There are many plants you can use to design your home garden including flowers, shrubs, trees and more, that will not contribute to your outdoor allergy symptoms . . . However, keep in mind that, even if your garden is 'allergy-free,' many of the pollens that affect you can travel via air to your yard from other gardens in the neighborhood or even from as far away as the next state. But there are intelligent and creative ways to make sure you minimize the allergens growing right in your own back yard.

Many plants 'mate' by releasing billions of pollen grains into the wind during the spring, summer, and fall months, including many grasses, trees, and bushes. These are the types of plants you want to avoid in your garden. Instead, you should consider plants that rely on insects for cross-pollination, which are known to have pollen grains that are much heavier and don't travel through the air quite as easily. Among these types of plants are several bright colored flowers, fruit trees and shrubs. Ask any nursery expert or a local horticulturalist to help you identify these types of plants and make a list of those you'd like to see in your garden plan."[34]

Avoid These Garden Plants If You Have Allergies[35]

- **Grasses**—Bermuda, Fescue, Johnson, June, Orchard, Perennial Rye, Redtop, Salt Grass, Sweet Vernal, Timothy
- **Shrubs**—Cypress, Juniper
- **Trees**—Alder, Ash, Aspen, Beech, Birch, Box Elder, Cedar, Cottonwood, Elm, Hickory, Maple, Mulberry, Oak, Olive, Palm, Pecan, Pine, Poplar, Sycamore, Walnut, Willow
- **Weeds**—Poison Ivy/Oak/Sumac, Cocklebur, Pigweed, Ragweed, Russian Thistle, Sagebrush

Consider These Garden Options, as They Are Less Allergenic[36]

- **Flowering Plants**—Begonia, Cactus, Chenille, Clematis, Columbine, Crocus, Daffodil, Daisy, Dusty Miller, Geranium, Hosta, Impatiens, Iris, Lily, Pansy, Periwinkle, Petunia, Phlox, Rose, Salvia, Snapdragon, Sunflower, Thrift, Tulip, Verbena, Zinnia
- **Grasses**—St. Augustine
- **Shrubs**—Azalea, Boxwood, English Yew, Hibiscus, Hydrangea, Viburnum
- **Trees**—Apple, Cherry, Chinese Fan Palm, Fern Pine, Dogwood, English Holly, Hardy Rubber Tree, Magnolia, Pear, Plum, Red Maple

"In addition to strategically selecting certain plants, other prevention tips include:

- When working outdoors, wear a face mask, hat, glasses, gloves and a long-sleeve shirt to reduce skin and nose contact with pollen.
- Since wood chips or mulch can retain moisture and encourage molds to grow, instead use gravel, oyster shell, or special plant groundcovers (vinca or pachysandra).
- Ask family members who don't have allergies to mow lawns and weed flower beds, or hire a landscaping firm.
- Keep grass cut low—maximum 2 inches high—to help keep stems of pollen from reaching too high into the wind.
- Be cautious about using hedges since their branches easily collect dust, mold, and pollen, and keep them pruned and thin.
- Keep the windows in the house closed while mowing and for a few hours afterward.
- Limit your gardening days to cool or cloudy days, and in the later afternoon or evening when pollen concentration in the air is generally lower.

- Immediately shower and change your clothes when you go back indoors and make sure to wash your hair to remove allergens trapped there."[37]

Clean Design Outdoor Living Guideline #4
Minimize Mold

There's no way to completely avoid mold spores outdoors—they are present in the air and land. But you can reduce your family's exposure to mold by keeping outdoor furniture and surfaces clean and dry. Choose outdoor furniture that can be washed easily, and store pieces in a dry place to avoid mold growth. Also, before using tables, chairs, and other outdoor surfaces, wipe them down with a water-bleach solution (use a mixture of one part bleach to four parts water in a spray bottle). Rinse with water and towel dry to prevent mold growth.

Clean Design Outdoor Living Guideline #5
Repel Insects Naturally

Mosquitoes are unwelcome participants in outdoor living. However, they can be repelled without the use of harsh chemicals. I recommend using natural, botanical-based, nontoxic insect repellent products.

Citronella candles can help keep mosquitoes away, although their smell may bother some asthma and allergy sufferers. Try including insect-repellent plants in your outdoor landscape, such as citronella grass, rosemary, scented geraniums, horsemint, marigolds, catnip, and ageratum (provided family members are not allergic to them). These plants emit fragrances that mosquitoes don't like. For

ALLERGY CONNECTIONS

Having certain plant allergies can raise your chances of being allergic to foods from related plant families, according to the American Academy of Allergy, Asthma & Immunology. Be on the lookout for these cross-reactions:[38]

If you're allergic to . . .	You may also be allergic to . . .
Ragweed	Fruits: bananas, cantaloupes, honeydew, watermelon Veggies: cucumbers, zucchini Other: chamomile tea, sunflower seeds
Birch pollen	Fruits: apples, apricots, cherries, kiwis, nectarines, peaches, pears, plums, tomatoes Veggies: carrots, peas, celery, green peppers, parsnips, potatoes Herbs: anise, caraway, cumin, dill, fennel, parsley Other: almonds, hazelnuts, peanuts, sunflower seeds, walnuts
Grass pollen	Fruits: kiwis, melons, oranges, tomatoes Veggies: celery

recommendations of other insect-repellent plants that thrive in your geographic area, check with an expert at your local garden center.

Another fantastic, nontoxic way of reducing mosquitoes in your outdoor living space is using an electric fan. Mosquitoes can't fly easily in a breeze, and fans help blow them away from your guests.

Although these natural insect repellent strategies can reduce the bother caused by mosquitoes and other insects, they may not work completely in areas with serious infestation. When mosquitoes are swarming in large numbers, or if insects that transmit disease such as West Nile virus are present in your area, consider staying indoors. Products containing DEET (or *N,N*-Diethyl-3-methylbenzamide or *N,N*-Diethyl-*m*-toluamide) are effective, but because of their chemical makeup, I consider them a last resort. Avoid using these products on your skin when possible by wearing long-sleeved pants and shirts.

No matter how hard you try, insect bites will still occur. You can manage bites by having natural, nontoxic anti-itch products on hand. If someone in your family has a serious insect-bite allergy and has been prescribed an Epi Pen by a health-care provider, be sure it's up to date and stored nearby in case it is needed.

Clean Design Outdoor Living Guideline #6
Stay Away from Smoke
The smoke produced by barbecue grills can trigger sneezing and wheezing in people with asthma and allergies. To manage smoke, cook with a gas grill, which produces less smoke than a charcoal grill—but remember, even a gas grill creates some smoke. Position the grill away from your family members and guests. If smoke is still a problem, remember this: You can have a festive, delicious meal outdoors *without* barbecuing. It's perfectly fine to serve meats cooked

GRILL SAFETY TIPS

- Keep your grill on level ground with good ventilation and at least 10 feet from your house's eaves.
- Always cook in an open space and keep a dry chemical fire extinguisher nearby.
- Keep kids and pets away from grills, which can stay hot for hours.
- Use tongs that are at least 14 inches long to avoid burning yourself.
- Use a meat thermometer to ensure that proper interior temperatures are met.
- Wear tighter clothing, pull back your hair, and wear closed-toe shoes while grilling.

Adapted from National Fire Protection Association, "Grilling Safety Tips," http://www .nfpa.org/safety-information/for-consumers/ outdoors/grilling/grilling-safety-tips.

indoors, along with luscious seasonal salads, fresh fruit, and chilled beverages.

Clean Design Outdoor Living Guideline #7
Leave the Outdoors Behind
When guests and family members enter your home after spending time out-doors, make sure they don't track in pollen, dust, dirt, and other allergens from the great outdoors. Have a space by the door where shoes can be taken off, and ask all visitors to wash their hands. People with allergies or asthma should consider using a neti pot in the eve-nings to wash pollen and other allergens out of the nose and sinus area.

RAGWEED: A MAJOR TRIGGER

Approximately 10 to 20 percent of Americans are allergic to ragweed,[39] according to the AAFA. Ragweed wreaks havoc in late summer, triggering asthma attacks in susceptible people and causing sneezing, wheezing, stuffy nose, itchy eyes, sore throat, and other symptoms. Ragweed is most common in the Eastern United States and the Midwest and often grows wild by riverbanks, roadways, and in vacant lots and open fields. Allergy and asthma sufferers should stay away from ragweed plants, although it's impossible to avoid ragweed pollen com-pletely, because winds can carry it as far as 400 miles. Ragweed pollen levels are highest shortly after dawn and between 10 a.m. and 3 p.m.[40]

SECTION II

WELLNESS GUIDE TO CLEAN DESIGN

Chapter 10

CLEAN DESIGN: WHAT IT IS, AND WHY IT MATTERS

"You can raise a strong child, or you can raise a child on strong medicine . . ."

—Dr. Williams, Austin, Texas, circa 1970

If you have ever rushed your child to the emergency room in the middle of the night because he or she could not breathe—or if you have ever found yourself gasping and wheezing, unable to fill your lungs with air—you know how important it is to avoid substances that trigger such symptoms. Unfortunately, our homes can contain a huge number of allergy and asthma triggers. The place that we think of as our ultimate shelter, our protection from the world, our safety zone, can be a major respiratory enemy. This is because the quality of the air we breathe in our homes—and our offices, schools, workplaces, and other

indoor spaces—can be quite poor. When you think of air pollution, you most likely imagine outdoor skies dirtied with smog and smoke. But for many of us, the air we routinely breathe indoors is less clean than the air outdoors. That is because it contains indoor air pollution—chemicals, gases, fumes, and other toxic substances that permeate the air—which can be ten times worse than what's found in outdoor air.

Exposure to indoor pollutants can cause or worsen many health problems. Asthma and allergies are among the most common, as are headaches; nausea; dizziness; fatigue; and irritation to the eyes, nose, and throat. Over time, exposure to pollutants can raise your risk of some kinds of cancer and serious diseases of the lungs, kidneys, and central nervous system. I know this sounds scary, because people don't want to think about the fact that the air in their home may not be safe. But ignoring the reality does not help, especially if you or someone in your family has asthma or allergies. The fact is, by making simple changes in your home environment—implementing the principles of Clean Design—you can reduce indoor air pollution, drastically improve your home's indoor air quality, and lower your exposure to allergy and asthma triggers and other airborne toxins.

SOURCES OF POOR AIR QUALITY

When mentioning toxins that contribute to poor indoor air quality, I am referring to the following substances that not only foul our indoor

air but also are major triggers of asthma and allergy symptoms:[41]

- **Combustion pollutants:** These are gases or airborne particles released by burning materials, especially fuels (gasoline, wood, kerosene, coal, charcoal, heating oil, and natural gas). They enter a home's air when furnaces, generators, space heaters, fireplaces, gas stoves, wood stoves, water heaters, dryers, motors, and other fuel-burning appliances are not properly vented.
  - **Carbon monoxide:** This colorless, tasteless, odorless gas is produced when fuels, tobacco, or other substances are burned. Although there is some carbon monoxide in the air we breathe, too much can prevent us from getting the oxygen we need.
  - **Nitrogen dioxide:** Like carbon monoxide, it cannot be seen or smelled. But when released into the air through the burning of fuel and other substances, it can irritate the respiratory system and promote infections.
- **Asbestos:** Commonly used in roofing and flooring materials and insulation prior to 1980, asbestos can release microscopic fibers into the air. When these fibers are breathed into the lungs, they can cause

scarring, lung cancer, and other lung diseases.

- **Volatile organic compounds (VOCs):** These are chemicals found in some types of paints, paint strippers, cleaning supplies, pesticides, office equipment, dry-cleaning solutions, and other chemicals used indoors. VOCs evaporate into the air during the use of and, in some cases, the storage of these products. They have been found to contribute to a wide variety of health problems.

- **Mold:** A fungus that grows in damp places, such as shower curtains, walls, drains, and refrigerator pans. Mold is a major allergy and asthma trigger.

- **Dust mites:** Microscopic bugs that live on our skin and in pillows, blankets, mattresses, upholstery, and stuffed animals. Their droppings and carcasses can trigger asthma and allergy symptoms. You cannot fully eliminate dust mites, but you can manage them.

- **Pet dander:** Microscopic flecks of skin shed by dogs, cats, rodents, birds, and any other animal with feathers or fur. Like mold and dust mites, it can trigger asthma attacks and allergic reactions.

- **Radon:** A radioactive gas that forms in soil and enters buildings through openings in floors and walls that come in contact with the ground. "Indoor radon exposure is estimated to be the second leading cause of lung cancer in the U.S."[42] [behind smoking] and the top cause of lung cancer among nonsmokers.

- **Secondhand smoke:** The smoke caused by the burning of tobacco products can cause or worsen asthma and is linked to ear infections, sudden infant death syndrome, and other health problems in children and adults. Plus the residue from secondhand smoke can linger in clothing, upholstery, and window treatments, and also cause yellowing of painted and furniture surfaces.

AVOIDING TRIGGERS

We have discussed the many ways that you can use Clean Design to decorate your home, and now you know why it is so important for people with allergies and asthma to avoid triggers.

I am not a doctor, and your health-care provider should be your primary source of advice about prevention and treatment of asthma, allergies, and other respiratory diseases. Over the years, I have educated myself on this topic, and I've learned quite a bit from being an ambassador for the Asthma and Allergy Foundation of America (AAFA)—the leading information provider for people with asthma and allergies in the United States. I'd like to share some basic information about asthma and allergies from my friends at AAFA.

Few people are aware that sixty million allergy and asthma sufferers are in the United States, which is one in five people.[43] This is an epidemic, and there is no cure for either condition; it affects people of all races, ages,

and genders. Conditions affecting sufferers can be managed with proper medical treatment; however, prevention strategies are just as critical. Unfortunately, asthma remains poorly controlled among many people, and if more people took preventative strategies to manage their home environment, they could be healthier and lead more active lives.

ALLERGIES

Allergies are "an overreaction of the immune system to a foreign protein substance, or 'allergen,' that is eaten, breathed into the lungs, injected, or touched."[44] Indoor and outdoor allergies are the most common—resulting in various symptoms, "such as coughing, sneezing, itchy eyes, runny nose and scratchy throat. In severe cases [allergic reactions can] also result in rashes, hives, lower blood pressure, difficulty breathing, asthma attacks, and even death."[45] Americans suffer from various types of allergies, including indoor/outdoor allergies and allergies to foods, drugs, latex, and insects.

Allergies can affect the respiratory system, the digestive system, the skin, and the eyes. People who have reactions to four or more triggers in multiple categories (pollen, dander, food, fumes, smoke, animals, etc.) may be diagnosed as "pan-allergic."

ASTHMA

"Asthma is a disease of the lungs in which the airways become blocked or narrowed, causing breathing difficulty."[46] During an asthma attack, the airways in the lungs become inflamed, swollen, and clogged with mucus. Asthma can cause shortness of breath, breathing trouble, coughing, wheezing, tightness in the chest, and other symptoms. Although asthma attacks are temporary, they can be severe, requiring emergency treatment to restore normal breathing. Asthma attacks typically happen when people are exposed to certain triggers. These triggers differ from person to person. For people with asthma, one of the best ways to manage it is to figure out what your triggers are, and then avoid them—and make sure a rescue inhaler is always available.

Asthma is commonly divided into two types: allergic and nonallergic asthma. *Allergic asthma* is an immune response "triggered by inhaling allergens such as dust mites, pet dander, pollens, mold, etc."[47] *Nonallergic asthma* is set off by "anxiety, stress, exercise, cold air, dry air, hyperventilation, smoke, viruses, or other irritants. In nonallergic asthma, the immune system is not involved in the reaction."[48] Although they have different triggers, these types tend to have similar symptoms.

CLEAN DESIGN: ELIMINATE OR MANAGE

Once you understand how asthma and allergies work—
basically, that they are reactions to substances in the
environment—it is easy to see why Clean Design makes so
much sense. Clean Design can create a home environment
that greatly reduces allergy and asthma triggers because
you are both managing the toxins that enter your home and
eliminating those that affect indoor air quality. Providing
a living space that supports respiratory health without
increasing your toxin load will automatically make you breathe

easier. Whether you or someone in your family has asthma or allergies, or you simply want to reduce your exposure to respiratory irritants, Clean Design allows you to turn your home environment into a purer, safer place with cleaner air and less indoor air pollution.

Although there are many strategies you can use to improve the air quality in your home, the two basic principles of Clean Design are really quite simple and can be summed up into two words: **eliminate** and **manage**.

To eliminate and manage means getting rid of as many sources of airborne toxins and indoor air pollution as possible, and actively managing those that cannot be fully eliminated, either through ventilation or extensive cleaning.

Here is an example of how to eliminate or manage allergy and asthma triggers: If you paint a room in your home, I recommend choosing a paint that has low– to no–volatile organic compounds (VOCs). In other words, I suggest you **eliminate** VOCs in the paint you use; however, if for some reason you must choose an oil-based paint product or if a strong paint remover must be used—I advise you to **manage** the product's risk. Use these steps: Vent fumes during use with an exhaust fan, live elsewhere while the product is used, and continue to ventilate the area well afterward.

Many consumers are not aware that dry-cleaning solvents contain ingredients, such as perchloroethylene (perc), that are believed to cause cancer.[49] Whenever possible, I recommend that you **eliminate** dry-cleaning fumes in your home by choosing clothing that does not need to be cleaned with potentially harmful solvents. However, I understand that zero dry cleaning is not an option for everyone. In that case, I urge you to **manage** dry-cleaning fumes in your house by storing dry-cleaned clothes in a well-ventilated area and keeping them far away from people with asthma and allergies.

By eliminating and managing the sources of indoor air pollution in your home, you can reduce allergy and asthma triggers and lower your family's exposure to airborne toxins. And by using Clean Design, you can help keep yourself and your loved ones safe and healthy, in a less toxic, wellness environment.

Chapter 11

SURFACES: COUNTERTOPS, WALLS, AND FLOORING

"My idea of superwoman is someone who scrubs her own floors."

—Bette Midler

One of the first things you notice when you enter a room is the walls. That is not surprising, since they typically account for more square footage than any other component in a home. The color, style, and texture of the walls set the tone for the entire room. You want your walls to make major design contributions, but you also want them to contribute to your family's good health. By making Clean Design–inspired choices about what you put on your walls and eliminating and managing asthma and allergy triggers in the products you use, you can create rooms that are beautiful and supportive of your family's good health.

The Clean Design goal for walls is to eliminate oil- and petroleum-based paints, stains, varnishes, and adhesives, which can contain toxic ingredients, and to choose water-, milk-, or latex-based products instead. If you must use trigger-inducing products, you can manage the impact on unsafe fumes related to indoor air quality by using them wisely and ventilating.

ECO-FRIENDLY PAINTS

When you open a typical can of paint, the first thing you notice—even before the color—is the smell. Paint's characteristic odor comes in large part from ingredients that contain volatile organic compounds (VOCs), which are chemicals that help paint adhere to walls. As soon as you pry off the lid of a paint can, the fumes in the paint immediately begin escaping into the air and into your lungs. This is referred to as off-gassing, and it is a big contributor to indoor air pollution.

Even in small amounts, airborne VOCs can trigger allergic reactions and asthma attacks; irritation to the eyes, nose, throat, and skin; nausea; headache; dizziness; fatigue; and other symptoms. Over time, exposure can cause significant health problems. Some of these compounds, including formaldehyde, benzene, and methylene chloride, are known carcinogens.[50]

VOCs from paint are released into the air during painting and, to a lesser degree, after the paint has dried. Not surprisingly, the highest levels of fumes enter the air when paint is fresh but can continue for months and perhaps even years. Ingredients containing VOCs are added to paints when the paints are manufactured. They may also be mixed in at the paint store during the custom color-tinting process.

VOCs do not just come from paint. They are found in many places in the home, including *some* kinds of: varnish, lacquers, paint strippers and solvents, wood preservatives, cleaning supplies, pesticides, building materials, furniture, synthetic carpeting, air fresheners, dry-cleaning solvents, office equipment (copiers, printers, correction fluids, permanent markers), art and craft materials, glues and adhesives, and photographic solutions.

Some numbers to give you an idea of how substantial this VOC release is, according to the Environmental Protection Agency (EPA)—indoor VOC levels are up to ten times higher than outdoors.[51] However, they can go much higher during and immediately following the use of paint and other similar products, such as varnishes. During and after paint stripping, for example, indoor VOC levels may be 1,000 times higher than they are outdoors.[52]

PAINTS TO CHOOSE

To protect your family, I recommend using paints that contain low to no VOCs. As consumers become more aware of the value of eco-friendly options, more manufacturers are creating products that meet this important goal, which limits off-gassing of paint fumes into a living space.

My favorite eco-friendly paints are Aura and Natura from Benjamin Moore.[53] Aura is a low-VOC paint. Its paint smell disappears within one hour of painting, and it is thick so that you rarely need to apply more than one coat, which saves on time and labor cost, especially if you are paying a professional painter. Natura contains zero VOCs, which means it is virtually odorless. Natura is slightly thinner than Aura, so it is more likely to require a second coat. But either one is an excellent choice for reducing your family's exposure to paint fumes.

Several other paint companies make low-VOC or milk paint products. Be sure to read the label (and check the manufacturer's website) to find out if the products really are low VOC. Some brands start out with a low-VOC

Q: IF MY WALLS WERE PAINTED WITH HIGH-VOC PAINT IN THE PAST, SHOULD I PAINT OVER THEM WITH LOW-VOC OR ZERO-VOC PAINT NOW, TO PROTECT MY FAMILY?

A: Unless you are redecorating, this probably is not necessary. Although paint continues to release VOCs long after it has dried, the majority of worrisome substances in paints enter the air during the first days and weeks after application. You can protect your family from VOCs in walls painted long ago by making sure your house is well ventilated.

It is more concerning to think about the possibility of having lead paint in your home. Lead can damage the human brain and nervous system and is particularly dangerous to children and pregnant women if they ingest lead-paint chips or breathe in its dust. Laws about using lead paint changed in 1978, so it is mainly a concern for people living in homes built and painted before that date. If you suspect you have lead paint on your walls, educate yourself about lead safety before painting, repairing, sanding, or skim-coating surfaces such as walls, ceilings, and woodwork. (An excellent place to start is the EPA website's lead information pages.) When any renovation of painted surfaces is called for, consider hiring a trustworthy contractor who has experience and certification in working with lead paint. Be sure you and your family vacate your home and remove all clothing and store your furnishings while the work is being done, and hire a professional cleanup crew to remove all dust after the job is completed. Any kind of repair work or renovation can cause lead paint dust to permeate your home even if protective cloths and covers are used, so a professional cleanup is essential.

base, but the tints added in the paint store contain substantial amounts of VOCs. *Be sure to read the fine print.*

If you must use paint products that contain high levels of VOCs—such as lacquers or metallic—make sure to manage their use carefully. Ventilate the area well during use and for several days after, and follow all manufacturer recommendations for safe use, ventilation, and storage. The best time to paint is when the weather is warm enough to

keep windows open. You can also use exhaust fans to pull fumes out of the house. If at all possible, anyone with asthma or allergies should spend a few days away from home when high-VOC products are used.

Keep in mind that paint strippers contain chemicals that must be strong enough to remove paint, and handling them incorrectly can be dangerous because they are high in toxins that are off-gassed into the air. If you really must strip paint from a surface, be sure to manage the process in a way that minimizes the effects on indoor air quality by closely following the directions on the product and ventilating carefully during use. Better yet, hire a trained, licensed professional who follows environmentally sound paint-removal protocols and regulations and who uses a reverse ventilation machine to remove fumes from your home. While the work is being done, leave your house and stay elsewhere for at least two days, especially if you have children.

Choose colors based on your personal taste, but keep in mind that in busy rooms with lots of furniture, it is nice to have the wall color serve as a background for the rest of the room rather than claiming too much attention for itself.

HEALTH-FRIENDLY WALL COVERINGS

If you prefer to use wall coverings rather than paint, it is important to choose wall coverings and adhesives that are safe and environmentally friendly, that do not off-gas, are easy to clean, and do not trigger asthma and allergies. Vinyl wall coverings can contain hazardous chemicals, including polyvinyl chloride (PVC), which contains VOCs, phthalates, and other cancer-causing substances. These chemicals can be in some wall coverings or in coatings added during manufacturing. The process of off-gassing can release these toxic substances into the air. Plus, over time as the wall covering ages, it may release toxic dust into the home environment. The paste used to attach wall coverings may also contain toxic ingredients.

In addition to off-gassing, wall coverings can trap moisture between the covering and the wall. Over time, this can foster the growth of mold and mildew, which are major allergy and asthma triggers.

To decorate safely with wall coverings, choose options made with natural, nonsynthetic materials such as cork, jute, grass cloth, silk, wood veneers, or paper. Be sure coverings are air permeable to prevent the growth of mold and mildew. And select an adhesive that is eco-friendly.

PAINT VIRTUALLY

The Benjamin Moore website (www.benjaminmoore.com) has a wealth of great information and tools that help you with your decorating choices. One great feature is its Personal Color Viewer, which allows you to "paint" a room virtually using any of Benjamin Moore's colors. It is a wonderful way to select options and to understand how wall color will look alongside a floor that is light, dark, or textured. You can even upload your own photo of a room, which allows you to envision how your room will look after it is painted.

FLOORING

Stylish floors can influence the character of any room, and the type of materials you choose for flooring is a crucial part of your Clean Design strategy in your home. Although flooring has a major impact on a room's look, choosing the right kind of flooring for your home is not just a style decision, especially when minimizing allergen triggers. Since dust accumulates on floors more than on any other surface, it makes great sense to install flooring that can be easily kept clean. Flooring materials should be as eco-friendly as possible and should contain minimal substances that trigger allergies, asthma, and other health problems.

Gleaming hardwood floors can add a feeling of rich warmth and fresh tradition; porcelain tile can modernize a space, giving it a contemporary, streamlined design with a bright, cool sensibility; while rugs provide a softening effect, often with a pattern or design that pulls a room together in a finished, complete way.

Like wall paint, certain flooring materials—such as wall-to-wall carpet, vinyl-back carpets, and vinyl flooring—may contain adhesives, backings, or sealants that emit VOCs. These products can release a chemical smell into the air for weeks or months after installation. Vinyl flooring is typically made with polyvinyl chloride (PVC), which is believed to be a human carcinogen and may also cause birth defects.[54] Synthetic carpets, which are typically made from petroleum-derived plastic fibers and may be installed with solvent-based adhesives, can be a substantial source of indoor air pollution. And for those with children, select rubber play mats (instead of vinyl!) for your children's playroom and to positively impact their respiratory health.

Your best flooring choices are all-natural materials that do not contribute toxins or allergens to your home environment. Here are some flooring options to consider.

Hardwood

In my mind, nothing beats hardwood for living areas. It is warm, rich, durable, and beautiful, and it maintains its value for a lifetime. When it is sustainably raised, harvesting timber from trees such as oak, pine, maple, pecan, and spruce has a minimal impact on the environment. Hardwood boasts a natural diversity of pattern and color unlike any other floor material. When you are making choices about installing a hardwood floor, look for wood that is certified by the Forest Stewardship Council (FSC; www.fsc.org), which ensures it came from sustainably managed forests. (This means that a tree is planted whenever another tree is cut down to manufacture flooring.) Visit their website for information on choosing products and to learn more about FSC's mission—to promote environmentally sound, socially beneficial, and economically prosperous management of the world's forests.

Hardwood flooring is harvested from timber of trees such as oak, pecan, maple, spruce, and pine. (It is renewable, but beware of harmful logging practices.) A budget-conscious product to consider is an engineered wood product from a company that maintains sustainable practices during the manufacturing process. Engineered hardwood flooring products work well with radiant heat because there is limited expansion and contraction.

Typically, polyurethane is used to finish floors. But polyurethane contains high levels of VOCs, so I suggest you avoid using

Q: MY EXISTING HARDWOOD FLOORS WERE FINISHED YEARS AGO WITH POLYURETHANE. SHOULD I REMOVE THE FINISH TO PREVENT OFF-GASSING INTO THE AIR?

A: Floors that were finished long ago are unlikely to off-gas into your home environment, so unless you are redecorating, removing existing varnish is not necessary. In fact, it may not be a good idea at all, because sanding varnished floors creates an enormous amount of dust that is difficult to contain even when rooms are sealed off with plastic and tape. It is best to leave floors as they are. When they do need refinishing, ventilate well, remove allergy and asthma sufferers from the premises for the duration of the refinishing, and choose a low-VOC or no-VOC finish such as linseed oil or a water-based product.

it and consider water-based stains/varnishes or linseed oil. If you must use polyurethane, manage risk by choosing a low-VOC formula, ventilating well, using an engineered floor, or consider having your family live elsewhere while floors are finished, especially if there are allergy and asthma sufferers in your family. Ventilation and avoidance should also be practiced when hardwood floors are sanded, because this produces lots of dust that can permeate all parts of a home even when care is taken to isolate and seal off the rooms with floors that are being refinished.

Some builders and homeowners opt to create custom flooring with hardwood salvaged from demolition sites such as homes, barns, and churches. Salvaging preexisting flooring is a lovely act of recycling that pays homage to the past while creating new flooring for future generations. Salvaged wood flooring can be used in planks or it can be recut into parquets arranged in unique, fascinating patterns.

Bamboo

Bamboo is an eco-healthy, hypoallergenic alternative to hardwood flooring, and it looks quite similar. However, bamboo is more sustainable than hardwood because it is a grass that can grow as much as several feet a day. The grass is harvested and then dried in a kiln. Bamboo stands up well to humidity, and mature species have the durability of hardwood. Be sure to install bamboo flooring using non-formaldehyde adhesives, and make sure an antiscratch UV coating is applied to prevent bleaching from the sun. For maintenance, you should ensure that high-heel shoes are removed, since certain bamboo is not as hard as regular wood.

Cork

Cork is a natural and resilient flooring option that is also great for sound minimization. Cork floors are made from the bark of cork oak trees, which are sustainably grown on plantations. Cork is a renewable resource—the bark returns after it is harvested and can be reharvested after seven to ten years. It is recyclable, biodegradable, and does not release toxic gas. Because it comes in tiles, it can be taken with you if you move. Chefs and pet owners like cork floors because they self-repair when cut by a dropped knife or scratched by claws. It is not recommended for use in basements where it may absorb moisture and be susceptible to mold.

Linoleum

Linoleum is back as an eco-healthy flooring option, although it has been rebranded as Marmoleum. It is durable, biodegradable, and comfortable, yet quiet when walked upon. This is not your grandmother's linoleum—there are fifty-plus newly created patterns and colors. It is made from natural materials such as felt, burlap, or canvas coated with linseed oil and comes in sheets, strips, or tiles. It is hypoallergenic and antistatic, meaning it repels dust and dirt; however, if you have chemical sensitivities, be aware of a natural off-gassing scent that will go away over time.

Concrete

Concrete slab foundations are being finished as floors, and the designs go way beyond the standard gray. Made from a mixture of cement, water, sand/gravel, and fly ash in some cases, it is an eco-material that is nearly impossible to damage and easy to clean. However, be aware of the natural tendency of concrete to develop fissures in its surface, which may mean that it must be sealed more frequently to prevent bacterial buildup.

Stone

Stone is a natural material that is virtually free of off-gassing. It creates an attractive surface that can easily be swept or mopped. There are many varieties of stone with different sizes, colors, and textures. Typically, stone includes marble, granite, or limestone, which are natural materials used in countertops, flooring, and wall cladding.

Tile

One of the oldest flooring materials, tile was first used over six thousand years ago. There are different kinds of tile available. Ceramic tile is made from clay that may or may not be glazed before being fired in a kiln. Porcelain tile is kiln-fired at a higher temperature and comes in multiple patterns, textures, and sizes—and some recent versions look like hardwood. Glass tile is made from new (clear or frosted) or recycled opaque artisan glass, which can be used on walls or floors. Setting tile in cement is the best option for indoor air quality and is more durable than adhesives, plus it works well with radiant heat systems.

Rugs and Carpet

Rugs and carpets add comfort and coziness to a home, and absorb sound. I recommend choosing rugs and carpets made of natural fibers that are affixed to natural fiber or rubber backings with eco-friendly adhesives. The healthiest carpets are those made from untreated 100 percent wool, cotton, sisal, hemp, or sea grass. Carpets that are healthy options will not off-gas with irritating or harmful fumes after installation. Overall limited use of wall-to-wall carpeting is recommended—and carpet tiles can be a better option.

When I was a child suffering from a wide range of allergies and constant asthma attacks, my parents pulled out all the wall-to-wall carpeting from our home and used ceramic tile, which made a big difference. Even if you vacuum a wall-to-wall carpet weekly with a powerful vacuum cleaner, you simply cannot remove all the dust, mold spores, dust mites, and other allergens that live in carpeting.

If you like the soft feeling that carpeting delivers, then consider the judicious use of natural-fiber throw rugs or carpet tiles placed over hardwood floors, tile, or other easy-to-clean, eco-friendly flooring. Easier to clean than wall-to-wall carpeting, they provide the warmth of carpeting without all the allergens and dust harbored in large areas of permanently installed carpeting.

I designed my daughter's nursery with FLOR carpet tiles because I wanted a soft surface on which she could crawl and learn to walk during her first few years of life, and later would have the option to pull the tiles up and revert to the hardwood floors. I selected a pattern that is whimsical, a reminder of the cartoon version of *Alice in Wonderland*. Remember the Cheshire cat with purple and lavender stripes, surrounded by the green tree leaves? It is a bit of whimsy, with a sophisticated checkerboard pattern, and a border of green.

FLOR MODULAR CARPET TILES

When it comes to carpet tiles, my favorite is FLOR (www.flor.com), which offers modular carpet tiles in a variety of colors and patterns. Using modular carpet tiles, you can design your own area rugs for the kitchen, nursery, or living room. No glue is needed for installation, so your existing floors will not be ruined. Instead, dots with the sticky side up connect each tile, which measures approximately 20 by 20 inches. One of the best things about FLOR carpet tiles is that they are washable with soap and water, which is helpful for families with babies and young children.

FLOR is a quick do-it-yourself project that can be installed over any level, dry surface—even vinyl. This is a great product for heavy-traffic rooms such as family rooms, and for those who are living in a rental apartment. These carpet tiles can be laid parquet style with ribbing in different directions and can enhance the upscale feel of any space. My baby nursery has hardwood floors, which we may eventually want to uncover after the toddler moments have passed. When that time comes, it will be easy to remove the FLOR tiles, and there will be no damage to the hardwood floors. If you decide to remove them, you can be eco-friendly when you discard the tiles, because the FLOR company allows you to return used tiles for recycling with a prepaid mailing label. I love that.

COUNTERTOPS

My favorite countertop brand is Silestone (www.silestoneusa.com) because it has an original patented formula that repels bacteria growth—thus making it an ideal surface for use in kitchens and bathrooms. Since it is a manmade quartz material, it does not have the natural fissures present in natural stone, which means that it requires less maintenance.

The product is scratch, stain, and acid resistant and comes in a huge number of textures and colors. There is always an option that can be suitable for a design project.

Chapter 12

FURNITURE AND FURNISHINGS

Having beautiful furniture and accessories is great, but the best part of design is ensuring that the space does not look like a mass-market retail showroom . . .

Furniture has many jobs to do, including being functional and comfortable. Seating should be practical and pleasant; beds must be supportive and sleep inducing; dressers and cabinets must be spacious enough to fit all of your belongings and treasures; and tables must stand ready for dinners, homework, and entertaining. Furniture should also be stylish: You want the pieces selected for your home to reflect and enhance your overall design and add beauty to your home. Finally, furniture should contribute to your Clean Design strategy and your family's good health by being easy to clean and not contributing toxins and allergens to indoor air.

It may sound like a tall order specifying furniture that is

Lighting Type	Pros	Cons
Compact fluorescent (CFL) bulbs	These low-voltage bulbs made in curious shapes are quite affordable. They use around 75% less electricity than a standard incandescent bulb.	These bulbs contain mercury in minute concentrations. When the bulbs are disposed of in landfills, the mercury can enter the landfills and leech into the ground and waterways. This poses a danger for marine life and for other wildlife and humans.
LED (light-emitting diodes) lighting	LED lights outlast incandescent bulbs by thirty times and can light a stairway or external area all night for less power than a single incandescent bulb uses in two hours. LEDs also produce more light per watt than standard incandescent bulbs.	In the past, the biggest barrier to their widespread adoption had been that the spectrum of light was too blue or too white, leading to an aquarium feel. Today, however, with modern innovations, color spectrum is improving and bulbs are now dimmable for some brands, which makes them perfect for enclosed spaces.
Low-voltage halogen	Halogen lights are more compact than incandescent bulbs and produce more lumens per bulb, although with some heat output. Typically, the bulbs allow a wide spectrum or a pinpoint spotlight. Because they can work at a very low energy use, a 50-watt low-voltage halogen bulb can produce the same lumens as a 125-watt bulb. Life is rated at approximately 2,000 hours.	Clear halogen bulbs produce harsh light—and are often used in fashion retail store windows. A better choice for the home is frosted or tinted halogen lights. They generate heat and should be limited in use for under-cabinet options or enclosed spaces because they can be a fire hazard or damage artwork with high temperatures or UV emissions. Do not handle with bare hands because the oil on your fingers can cause bulbs to weaken and break.
Xenon lights	Perfect for under-cabinet lighting, cove, and accent lighting because they give off such a bright light. These bulbs last longer than halogen bulbs and are more efficient. Life is rated at 10,000 hours.	Do not use in an enclosed space due to heat emission.
Solatube	This is a skylight-like passive lighting device that allows light to enter places where natural light cannot reach. Through a system of mirrors and reflectors, light enters a dome-shaped prism on the roof of a building and is propelled into an interior space without any heat or UV rays. For a center-hall home, this is a way to add more natural light during the day and save on electricity. In a location such as a closet, it eliminates the peak demand during morning rush hour.	Low-cost product that is great on a new construction project. Can be costly to install on a retrofit, although energy savings defray the expenditure over time.

Lighting Type	Pros	Cons
Fiber optics	These lights, which are becoming increasingly popular with consumers, use up to eight times less energy than standard incandescent bulbs. Additionally, they do not generate heat, which can help lower cooling bills. Plus, for those who have precious artwork or autographs, fiber optic lighting is good because it does not emit UV rays that can cause colors to fade. Depending on the source light, fiber optic light systems can emit 90 lumens per watt without heat emission, while a standard incandescent light produces 15 lumens per watt.	Fiber optic prices have been high, but they are coming down, making them an increasingly good choice for use in walkways and as task lighting.
Night-lights	Nighttime lighting is important for all members of the family but especially for older people. I recommend generous use of night-lights. The most eco-friendly options are LED lights, which use less than one watt of power and last up to 30,000 hours. Some models are light sensitive, so they automatically turn off when ambient light reaches a certain level. And the bulbs will not shatter if dropped. LED night lights do it all—keep your family safe while costing little to operate, generating no heat, and keeping waste out of landfills because they last for years.	LED options are recommended, as options using incandescent bulbs can overheat, causing them to melt and cause fire. Babies and small children may play with floor models, and bulbs can be a choking or breakage hazard. Only install in well-ventilated areas with cool-touch LED options.
Wind-up lights	Eco-friendly wind-up LED or xenon flashlights are ready anytime and never go dim for want of batteries. A quick crank of the handle allows approximately eight minutes of light, although some smaller handbag-sized versions can last for hours. This is a great option instead of plugging in a rechargeable flashlight.	Not recommended for people with arthritis.

Chapter 15

CLEANING TOOLS AND TIPS

"Cleaning your house while your children are still growing up is like shoveling the sidewalk before it stops snowing."

—Phyllis Diller

Clean Design is a two-step process: first, designing, decorating, and furnishing your home in a nontoxic, allergy- and asthma-friendly way; and second, keeping your home clean by eliminating and managing allergens, asthma triggers, dirt, dust, pollen, and toxins that enter your home and collect in every room. In this chapter, we will discuss products and the best ways to keep your home clean. Effective, efficient cleaning comes down to knowing what, when, and how to clean. Once you have that figured out you can fly through your home and have it cleaned in no time.

When you decorate your home using the principles of Clean Design, you may spend *less* time cleaning than

previously. That is because rooms are designed for fast, frequent cleaning. Quick-mopping a hardwood or tile floor takes much less time than thoroughly vacuuming wall-to-wall carpet, for example. Chasing dust bunnies out from under a sofa is much simpler when the sofa does not have heavy skirts, and less clutter and fewer trinkets means easier dusting. Following the principles of Clean Design will allow you to create a living space that will make your lifestyle easier, and toxins will be managed—which makes life healthier for everyone in the family.

BEST CLEANING SUPPLIES

Remember certain commercials for heavy-duty forest-scented cleaning products that basically said a room was not clean unless it smelled like that? Many people—friends, clients, even people in the wellness profession—assume that the smell of "clean" is a sharp odor of ammonia, bleach, or other harsh chemicals. Do not believe it!

The scent of "clean" does not involve fumes from chemical solvents or odors from artificially scented products. Clean Design makes those odiferous cleaners obsolete. The truth is that in many cases, water with a little bleach, lemon juice, white vinegar, baking soda, or even toothpaste can be the best "cleaning product," and these leave little or no scent behind. When you need extra help, select cleaners that are labeled "natural," "hypoallergenic," or "non-toxic." Remember, in a home with allergy and asthma sufferers, you want to use products that do not trigger symptoms.

Depending on your family members' individual needs or sensitivities, even "natural" cleaners can trigger symptoms—for example, if someone is allergic to lemons or tea tree oil, those scented products may trigger an allergic reaction, even if the products are 100 percent essential oils that are free of toxins and harsh chemicals.

Some of the best cleaners are already in your kitchen—and a grandmother's secret is sometimes the least toxic option, so I will share a few priceless tips from my grandmother.

GRANDMOTHER'S SIMPLE CLEANING SOLUTIONS

Product	Cleaning Checklist
Baking soda	✓ Toilet bowl rings can be removed if every week you sprinkle toilet interior with 1 cup of baking soda, and let sit for thirty minutes. Then spray white vinegar to moisten. Scrub with bowl brush and flush. ✓ Glass shower doors can be cleaned if you sprinkle some on a damp sponge and wipe down the glass. Rinse well and dry. ✓ Sluggish showerheads can be caused by mineral deposits that can be removed if you detach showerhead and soak for an hour in ½ cup of baking soda mixed with 1 cup of vinegar. Reattach and then run hot water through showerhead for five minutes. ✓ Remove burned food from pan and pot bottoms. Sprinkle over burned areas, add hot water, and soak overnight. Scrub in morning. ✓ Polish silver. Make a paste with ⅔ cup baking soda and ⅓ cup water. Rub onto silver with clean cloth. Rinse.
Lemon	✓ Food storage container stains can be removed if you squeeze lemon juice into container and add baking soda. Rub into stains. Soak overnight. Repeat if necessary. ✓ Remove refrigerator odors by cutting a lemon in half and placing it inside. Takes approximately two days to fully remove odors. Change weekly. ✓ Polish wood furniture with 1 teaspoon of lemon juice mixed into one pint of mineral oil. Rub on furniture. ✓ Clean windows and mirrors by putting 2 tablespoons of lemon juice to 1 cup of water into a spray bottle. Spray and wipe. ✓ Remove rust stains from cotton clothing fabrics. Add lemon juice to stain; sprinkle with cream of tartar and rub into fabric. Let sit until stain is gone. Wash clothing item.
Toothpaste	✓ Cleans crayon marks off walls. ✓ Whitens tile grout. ✓ Cleans grease catchers on stove.
Vinegar—white distilled	✓ Removes bad odors from a room—place an open bowl full of vinegar overnight and the following morning the smell will be gone. ✓ Remove non-oily stains from carpets with 1 teaspoon of liquid detergent and 1 teaspoon of white distilled vinegar in a pint of water. Use a towel or brush to remove stains and blot dry. Repeat as needed. ✓ Remove rings from wet glasses on wood furniture by mixing equal parts of olive oil and white distilled vinegar. Rub following the direction of the wood's grain. ✓ Deter ants by washing counters, cabinets, and floors with an undiluted solution of white distilled vinegar ✓ Stainless steel streaks can be removed; rub following the direction of the grain and try in a corner first. ✓ Prevent mildew in shower by spraying vinegar on shower walls or curtains. ✓ Remove stickers with vinegar. Wet sticker with undiluted vinegar and let sit for ten minutes, then remove.

CLEANING TIPS FOR EVERY ROOM OF THE HOUSE: A CHECKLIST FOR SUCCESS

Room	Cleaning Checklist
Bedrooms and living areas	✓ Remove bedding from mattress. Wash sheets, pillowcases, and pillow covers in warm or hot water. Wash duvet covers and mattress covers at least twice a year in hot water with bleach. ✓ Vacuum upholstered furniture. Be sure to get the vacuum hose attachment in as deep as possible behind cushions and within folds to eliminate dust mites and other allergens that can hide deep inside cushions. ✓ Clean dust from hard surfaces using a damp cloth. Wipe dust from walls, ceilings, moldings, headboards, ceiling fan blades, windows, sills, shelving, cabinets, storage boxes, and the tops of doors and shutters. ✓ Clean closets with focus on shelves and in corners. ✓ Clean hardwood flooring with a minimally damp mop or electrostatic mop to ensure dust removal. ✓ If you have wall-to-wall carpeting, vacuum weekly (or more often, if you have pets or lots of foot traffic in your home) with a HEPA-filter vacuum. I also recommend having it professionally steam cleaned three to four times per year using Stanley Steemer, an AAFA-certified professional steam-cleaning service. For more information, go to www.aafa.org/certified. ✓ Skip the artificial sprays and make a natural air freshener by combining 1 teaspoon baking soda and 1 teaspoon lemon juice with 2 cups hot water. (Use a new spray bottle or one that has never contained chemicals. Remember that even if you have rinsed out the bottle, residual chemicals might remain.) You can also zest a lemon or orange for a refreshing scent, or include cinnamon and cloves for a warm, welcoming aroma. ✓ Once a year, give rooms a top-to-bottom cleaning. Remove everything from the room (including furniture and clothing) as though you were moving out. Mop or steam clean the flooring and focus on corners. Use a mixture of one part bleach to four parts water in a spray bottle and spray lightly on a cloth. Wipe the walls and corners near floor. ✓ Wash all clothing items before replacing in closet. (This is a good time to donate unworn clothes and accessories to charitable causes.)
Laundry room	✓ Clean dryer lint traps after every load. Clean the dryer's exterior vent regularly to prevent fires from starting. ✓ To prevent mold growth, clean front-load washers regularly using a mixture of one part vinegar or bleach to one part water. ✓ Leave the door open between loads to prevent the growth of mold.
Bathrooms	✓ Always close the toilet lid before flushing, because flushing can cause tiny droplets of bacteria-laden water to enter the air and come to rest on surfaces nearby. For this reason, store toothbrushes, face cloths, and other items away from the toilet. ✓ Replace a vinyl shower curtain liner with a nylon liner. ✓ Wash your shower curtain liner if it is nylon at least once annually. ✓ Regularly clean tub, tiles, and shower walls to limit mold/mildew growth. ✓ Use all-natural, nontoxic cleaners, especially in enclosed spaces.
Windows	✓ Use newspaper to clean your windows. Newsprint is a cousin to paper towels, but its high absorbency makes it more effective and will leave windows sparkling. Newspaper is also recyclable. But be careful—the one downside of newspaper is that wet ink can stain wood moldings, so use extra caution. ✓ Use nontoxic, hypoallergenic, natural window cleaners—or better yet, use warm water with a couple of drops of liquid dish soap.

Room	Cleaning Checklist
Kitchen	✓ Use microfiber cloths instead of paper towels on floors, tile, and countertops. They do a great job sanitizing and can be reused. ✓ Change the filter for refrigerator water and ice maker every six to twelve months to prevent bacterial growth. Empty water weekly from an older refrigerator drain pan. ✓ Pull out your appliances (stove, refrigerator, dishwasher) once a year and vacuum up the crumbs and dust that collect under and behind them. ✓ If there are any holes in the floor or walls, cover and seal them to keep pests out. ✓ Change the filter on the exhaust fan or stove hood periodically. ✓ Keep your sink disposal smelling fresh by adding citrus peels and ice cubes. Do this once a month while running the water and turning on the disposal. (It will make a lot of noise!) After the noise ceases, turn off the disposal and continue to run the water for thirty seconds. Voila . . . clean, citrus scent from your sink! ✓ Run your dishwasher at least once a week, and clean the trap to prevent mold growth. If you have a drawer-style dishwasher that leaves a small amount of water in it after a cycle in the tub and you do not use it frequently, dry out the water using an absorbent towel. (This is especially important when you go on vacation.) Follow the manufacturer's instructions regarding emptying and cleaning the dishwasher's trap. When you go on vacation, do not leave dishes in the dishwasher for several days with the door shut, because mold can grow on them. ✓ It may sound odd, but it is a good idea to "clean" your dishwasher every three months. Run an empty cycle and add 2 cups of white vinegar (do not use bleach!). At the end of the cycle, open the door for thirty minutes to let the dishwasher air out and dry any water residue. ✓ Do not forget to clean your can opener. Bacteria can grow on food residue that clings to both manual and electric can openers. Wipe the cutting circle clean after each use. To clean thoroughly, use a wet toothbrush coated with baking soda (or run manual can openers through the dishwasher).
Sinks	✓ Sinks can be some of the dirtiest, germiest places in our bathrooms and kitchens, so be sure to clean yours regularly. ✓ Stainless steel sinks: Use a nontoxic all-purpose cleaner or distilled white vinegar on a sponge or cloth. Never use steel wool or abrasive cleaners. Spot clean with baking soda on a damp sponge or cloth and always scrub "with the grain." ✓ Porcelain sinks: Use baking soda on a damp sponge or cloth and avoid abrasive cleaners. Or use a cream cleanser or nonabrasive cleanser to assist with difficult stains. ✓ Composites/quartz sinks: Use cream cleansers or distilled white vinegar on a sponge or cloth.
Cleaning tools	✓ Be careful using sponges; they can harbor germs and spread them on countertops and dishes. If you use sponges, replace them monthly and have a different sponge for every room in the house. ✓ Clean sponges regularly in the dishwasher or by submerging them in a bowl of boiling water with a sprinkle of baking soda. ✓ Mops can also collect bacteria. For that reason, replace fabric or sponge mops regularly. ✓ Replace vacuum bags/filters frequently and use a HEPA-filter vacuum that has a bagless feature. Check the manufacturer's instructions. ✓ Replace air conditioner/heater filters on a quarterly basis.

- Make sure all mattresses, box springs, and pillows are encased in dust mite–proof covers.
- Choose upholstery that can be cleaned easily, or select wood or leather furniture instead. If you have upholstered furniture, vacuum it thoroughly each week using a HEPA-filter vacuum.
- Remove dust from furniture, windowsills, and other surfaces at least once a week using a water-dampened cloth. Do not use feather dusters or other cleaning tools that simply move dust around.

FACTS ABOUT DUST MITES

Here is some information about dust mites from the experts at the Asthma and Allergy Foundation of America (AAFA). This may be too much information for you, but the truth is, the more you know about allergens and asthma triggers in your home, the better equipped you are to eliminate or manage them effectively:

Too small to be seen with the naked eye, a dust mite measures only about one-quarter to one-third of a millimeter. Under a microscope, they can be seen as whitish bugs. Mites are technically not insects but arthropods, like spiders, with eight legs.

Mites are primitive creatures that have no developed respiratory system and no eyes. They spend their lives moving about, eating, reproducing, and eliminating waste products. A mite's life cycle consists of several stages, from egg to adult. A female may lay as many as 100 eggs in her lifetime. Depending on the species, it takes anywhere from 2 to 5 weeks for an adult mite to develop from an egg. Adults may live for 2 to 4 months.

Dust mites thrive in temperatures of 68 to 77 degrees Fahrenheit and relative humidity levels of 70 percent to 80 percent. There are at least 13 species of mites, all of which are well adapted to the environment inside your home. They feed chiefly on the tiny flakes of human skin that people normally shed each day. These flakes can work their way deep into the inner layers of furniture, carpets, bedding, and even stuffed toys. These are the places where mites thrive. An average adult person may shed up to 1.5 grams of skin in a day . . . enough to feed 1 million dust mites.

Unless you live in Antarctica or in an extremely dry climate, there is probably no practical way to completely rid your home of dust mites.[59]

You can take action to reduce your exposure to mites. Remember that all spaces where humans exist have dust mites, so it does not mean that your house is not clean.

- Dust mites prefer a humid environment, so keep humidity levels in your home below 60 percent (or lower) by using a dehumidifier or air conditioner.
- Clean floors and rugs (including under the bed and in closets) at least once a week using a HEPA-filter vacuum.
- Wash your child's stuffed toys in warm water, and be sure they are completely dry to prevent mold growth. If they cannot be washed, freeze them for 24 hours in a ziplock bag at least once a month; shake the toy before opening the bag so dead mites fall to bottom of bag. Remove the stuffed toy for playtime and a lower level of wheezing and sneezing.

RULE OF THREE FOR PILLOWS

For pillows, follow the Clean Design "rule of three": Wash your pillow cover every three weeks, wash your pillow every three months, and replace your pillow every three years (at a minimum).

Chapter 16

TRIGGER SAFE: HOW TO ELIMINATE AND MANAGE THE TOP TEN ALLERGY AND ASTHMA TRIGGERS

Being pan-allergic means you are sensitive to everything—from food to animal dander to dust to chemicals—and the only way to know is to get tested or to have a reaction . . . the unfortunate thing about trial and error is the possibility of an anaphylactic reaction . . .

Clean Design means recognizing the top ten sources of allergen and asthma triggers—and from indoor pollutants to environmental toxins, you can control and safeguard your family's health during the design process for your home. In this chapter, you will learn the best ways to eliminate and manage the top ten sources of allergens and asthma triggers.

TRIGGER #1: TOBACCO SMOKE

Tobacco smoke—the most common asthma trigger—is dangerous for everyone, but is especially harmful for people

sick when exposed to mold, and "other recent studies have suggested a potential link of early mold exposure to development of asthma in some children."[62] Mold, a type of fungus (and relative of yeast and mushrooms), is a living organism that can grow in damp places and reproduces by forming microscopic spores that disperse into the environment via air and growth on surfaces.

There is nothing you can do to keep mold spores out of your indoor air. But you can take steps to make your home inhospitable to airborne mold. Mold spores float around, and when they land on a surface, they can begin to grow if there is moisture to continue their life cycle. Mold spores love wet surfaces and humid air—especially air that has a humidity of 60 percent or greater. Once mold spores make themselves at home on a surface, they form colonies that spread and send out more spores. As long as the living conditions are suitably moist, mold continues to spread. On a visible surface, such as a bathroom ceiling or a basement wall, a mold colony typically looks like a splotchy spray or spots of black or green dirt that may or may not have a noticeable smell. However, mold can also be pinkish or yellowish, as it often is on a perpetually damp shower curtain liner. And mildew, another kind of fungus, tends to be white and powdery, or a dark, greenish spot on the floor or corner in a bathtub.

Mold can grow almost anywhere if there is a source of moisture, including roofs, windows, pipes, ceiling tiles, heating ducts, humidifiers, refrigerator drain pans, furniture, walls, wallpaper, insulation, carpet, drywall, upholstery, shower curtains, and clothing. A hearty organism, mold can grow in some surprising places, including books—which is why old bookstores and libraries often have a musty odor.

Mold and mold spores can cause a variety of health problems in people who are sensitive to them, including asthma attacks, allergy symptoms, coughing, wheezing, and irritation of the eyes, skin, throat, and nose. Mold exposure can also trigger serious infections in people with chronic lung illnesses. And it is imperative that you create an environment that makes it difficult for mold spores to grow by taking these steps:

- **Lower your home's humidity.** Because mold grows best in environments with high humidity, the best way to prevent mold spores from finding a place to grow and flourish is to keep your home's humidity low. Experts recommend a target home humidity rate of 30 to 60 percent— the lower, the better. Use humidity monitors to check moisture levels throughout your house. And consider purchasing a dehumidifier that will wick moisture out of the space; also purchase a dehumidifier unit for your basement/laundry area.
- **Ventilate well.** Exhaust fans in bathrooms, kitchens, and other damp rooms can expel dampness from your home. Be sure exhaust fans vent outside your home and not into the attic, crawlspace, between walls, or into the basement. Clothes dryers should also be vented outside if

at all possible. If you have a ventless clothes dryer that uses infrared technology, be sure to follow the manufacturer's maintenance recommendations and clean filters regularly. If you do not have exhaust fans in bathrooms and other humid spaces, open a window while the shower is running and encourage your family members to take brief showers.

- **Monitor your home when storms strike.** After a rainstorm, check basement and attic areas to determine whether moisture has entered your home. Find the source and address it right away to prevent mold buildup within the walls. If water has entered your home, dry it right away—within 24 to 48 hours or sooner. Remove carpeting, drywall, and flooring that has been damaged by water, and use a dehumidifier for at least two weeks to thoroughly dry the space, especially in basements. If ceiling tiles or drywall get wet, it is best to remove them and replace them to ensure there is not a quiet enemy growing behind your building materials.

- **Manage moisture in the basement.** Typical basements have some amount of moisture due to soil, runoff, or age of foundation. If your basement tends to flood or leak when you have heavy rain, consider installing drains, sump pumps, or have a dehumidifier in the space set to turn on when humidity rises above 30

Q: WHAT IS THE BEST WAY TO REMOVE MOLD?

A: You have several choices. Start with soap and water, and if that does not work, use a bleach solution (1 cup of bleach mixed in 1 gallon of water). If you need the big guns, turn to a commercial mold-removal product. To protect yourself, your family, and your home environment while removing mold, be sure to manage risk by closely following the directions on any mold-removal product. Ventilate the area well, and wear a mask, protective eyewear, and nonporous gloves. If the area to be cleaned is larger than 10 square feet, consider getting help from a mold-removal professional.

to 60 percent. If you have a finished basement, consider using paperless drywall because mold cannot live on it. Also ensure that any lower-level plumbing fixtures are regularly checked for leaks, including the wax seal on your toilet or shower (if you have one in the basement) and the tubing from your washer or a water-removal system that prevents water from collecting in your basement. If the walls in a humid room or basement are covered with porous materials such as wallpaper, wallboard, plasterboard, or paneling, consider removing it, since mold can grow unseen on walls beneath wall coverings. Also in the basement, keep sinks and tubs dry and clean, wash garbage pails often, and avoid leaving piles of damp towels or wet laundry in the washer, dryer, or elsewhere.

- **Be on the lookout for standing water.** Check pipes, sinks, ceilings, roofs, and floors for leaks, and repair leaks as soon as you find them. Anyplace there is moisture, mold can grow. Most people forget to check receptacles that collect water such as refrigerator trays and dehumidifier bins. Empty and wash them regularly.

TRIGGER #4: POLLEN

Managing your family's exposure to pollen, a potent asthma and allergy trigger, is a key principle of Clean Design. More people are allergic to pollen than to anything else in our environment. Pollen is a dusty powder produced by plants, grasses, and trees as part of their reproductive process. People with pollen allergies (also known as hay fever, seasonal allergies, or seasonal allergic rhinitis) suffer with a runny nose, nasal congestion, watery eyes, and/or sneezing. Less commonly, they can experience more serious allergic reactions including hives, trouble breathing, and swelling of the throat.

You may notice clumps of powdery pollen on bright-colored flowers, but that is not the pollen that causes most of the trouble for people with allergies. People tend to be bothered more by pollen from trees, grasses, and weeds, because these plants produce enormous amounts of fine, dry pollen that is released into the atmosphere. Wind carries pollen great distances, so even if you do not have allergenic plants in your immediate surroundings, you can still be exposed to their pollen.

The best advice for people with pollen allergies and pollen-induced asthma is to stay indoors with the windows closed when pollen levels are high, and ventilate using air conditioners with clean filters. Restrict outdoor activities to late afternoon or right after it rains, when pollen levels are lower. But even if you stay away from outdoor pollen, it can find ways to get into your indoor environment as well. To manage pollen in your home, take these steps:

- Do not dry your clothes on an outdoor clothesline.
- After spending time outdoors, wash clothes or put them in the dryer without heat to remove pollen from them. Ask family members to do so as well.
- Bathe before going to bed to rinse pollen off your body, and shampoo your hair.
- Place the clothes you wore in a covered laundry hamper outside of your bedroom.
- Wash your pillow cover frequently.
- Wash your arms, hands, and face after coming in from outdoors.
- If you have wall-to-wall carpeting, steam clean it regularly to remove pollen that can easily become trapped in carpet fibers.
- Use a HEPA-filter vacuum to ensure your space is cleaned more efficiently.

- Remove your shoes when you enter your home.

TRIGGER #5: DUST

There is no way to keep dust out of our homes. But we can use Clean Design on our rooms with two goals in mind: First, to minimize the surfaces where dust can collect, and second, to make it as easy as possible to remove dust from a room.

Dust is a fine powder that floats in the air and lands on surfaces in a room. It is made of small particles of all the things in our world that can become airborne: soil, sand, plant pollen, hair from animals and humans, skin cells from animals and humans, fibers from fabric, body part waste materials from dust mites, and other residue floating around in the atmosphere. And if possible, try to keep books stored in hallways or other spaces outside your sleeping area.

No matter what it is made of, dust is an enemy of people with asthma and allergies because it irritates the respiratory system and may trigger an immune reaction. When the body mounts an immune response, its goal is to repel "invaders" such as dust from your system. It does so by directing your respiratory system to sneeze, cough, wheeze, and produce extra tears and mucus, all in an effort to rid your body of whatever it is fighting.

TRIGGER #6: CLOTHING

Our skin is our largest organ, so it makes sense to try our best to keep toxic chemicals away, and for these reasons, it is important to manage triggers by washing all clothes, especially synthetics, before wearing them. Some new clothes contain chemicals such as formaldehyde, which is thought to prevent wrinkling and mildew growth.[63] Toxins can also be released by synthetic clothing such as rayon, acetate, nylon, polyester, and acrylic—and it is often thought that cotton or silk is a better option for anyone focused on Clean Design.

You probably do not think of your clothing as a source of indoor air pollution, but it very well can be, because chemicals in dry-cleaned clothing can also off-gas into the air, contributing to indoor air pollution. Dry-cleaned clothing can contain perchloroethylene (perc), a solvent that has been shown to cause cancer in animals and is believed to be a human carcinogen as well.[64] When you wear dry-cleaned clothing, and while it hangs in your closet, it can release perc into the air.

I have found that many of my "dry clean only" clothes can be successfully hand washed. Although some dry-cleaners do claim to use "green" solvents, experts disagree on whether these alternatives really are much better for the environment and our health. I recommend buying clothes that do not require dry cleaning. And if you must dry-clean your clothes, hang them in a well-ventilated area for several days before wearing them.

TRIGGER #7: CLEANING SUPPLIES AND HOUSEHOLD PRODUCTS

Cleaning supplies and other household products have the potential to enter the air and make people sick. They can be especially unsafe for family members with allergies and asthma. You can be safe with cleaning supplies and household products, but my advice is to have as few of these products in your home as possible.

It is an easy bet that if you were to take a look under your sink or in the storage areas in your basement or garage, you would find many products you no longer need. So often we buy a product, use it once or twice, and leave it in our storage areas for years or even decades. I recommended that everyone review the chemicals in their homes for proper disposal because plastic containers deteriorate, which can allow fumes to escape from containers. Be sure to dispose of these products properly—check with your municipality's waste disposal office to find out the best way to throw them away, and look for your community's annual or quarterly waste disposal days. Take these days as an opportunity to rid your home of unneeded chemicals. For the products that remain, here are some tips on how to handle them safely:

- Read and follow all instructions related to the safe use and storage of household products.
- Always ventilate the area when using household products—open windows, use an exhaust fan to remove fumes, and do not mix household products unless advised to do so in the directions. Harmful chemical reactions can occur when products are mixed.
- Store household products away from children in a well-ventilated place. Be sure the containers are tightly closed to help prevent fumes from leaking out.
- When buying household products, choose small containers and discard after using rather than storing them in your home for months or years. Sure, you will probably pay a higher price per ounce for a small container, but it is worth it for the savings to your family's health and indoor air quality.
- Check your household product storage area frequently and discard any products that are old or unneeded or whose containers may not be adequately sealed.

TRIGGER #8: VERMIN

In addition to being unsanitary, cockroaches, mice, rats, and other vermin leave behind droppings that are major triggers for asthma and allergies. To protect your home from vermin, keep it free of crumbs, drips, and other food waste and repair holes in walls, cracks in floors, tears in window screens, and other entry points that roaches, bugs, and other vermin use to gain access to your home.

If you have cockroaches or other pests, hire professional extermination services to kill them, and check with your health-care provider if you have questions about extermination products. Because vermin can be hard to eradicate, it is best to work with pest control experts. For ongoing bug and vermin control, be cautious about using off-the-shelf products for do-it-yourself application, because improper use or lack of ventilation can create a more toxic environment in your home and can trigger reactions in family members with chemical sensitivities. If you must use a chemical pesticide, always ventilate at least 12 hours (or longer, if the manufacturer recommends it) after using an off-the-shelf product.

TRIGGER #9: ODORS

Although they seem harmless enough, scented products—soaps, shampoos, perfumes, lotions, cleaning products, deodorants, and even nail polish, to name a few—can be a big symptom trigger for people with allergies and asthma. Avoid bringing these products into your home, and ask visitors not to use them. Additionally, manage your use of air fresheners, avoiding plug-in fragrance boxes and scented candles.

TRIGGER #10: WOOD SMOKE

Fireplaces can be a beautiful focal point in a room. Unfortunately, using them to burn wood is not a great idea for allergy and asthma sufferers, because the smoke and

gases released by the flames can trigger asthma attacks and respiratory allergies. The same can happen with wood stoves. Your fireplace can add style to your home without contributing smoke and allergens to indoor air. (See chapter 2 "Living Rooms" for more information about using your fireplace to beautify your rooms without ever lighting a fire.)

Chapter 17

BUILDING ENVELOPE: HEALTHIER AND NONTOXIC OPTIONS

*Detoxification means limiting the exposure to toxic things and
allowing the body to rest in a place of sanctuary.*

Although there are many strategies you can use to improve the air quality in your home, the basic principles of Clean Design are to eliminate or actively manage the sources of indoor air pollution and allergy and asthma triggers in your home. But remember, no matter how "clean" and eco-friendly your home furnishings are, you must have proper ventilation, too, because it allows you to manage your home's air quality. Through the smart use of ventilation, you can remove many of the toxins and allergens that get released into your home's air.

Inadequate ventilation is thought to be a contributing

factor in "sick building syndrome."[65] This term is used to describe situations in which a particular house or building causes negative health symptoms in the people who live, work, or spend time in it. Inadequate ventilation contributes to poor air quality, and improving ventilation can help. We also have tighter building envelopes, which means that the insulation and windows let less air into our spaces, so we must ensure that the toxins we use in our homes, such as chemicals, have a way to escape.

Adequate ventilation brings fresh air indoors and sends indoor pollutants, airborne emissions, and gases out of your home. There are several ways to ventilate your home. Which one you choose at any particular time depends on what is going on at the time indoors and outdoors.

Here are my recommendations for Clean Design ventilation strategies that help eliminate and manage airborne allergens and asthma triggers in your home.

Clean Design Ventilation Strategy #1
Open the Windows

The easiest way to ventilate is also the simplest—opening windows will let stale air out and fresh air in. When outdoor air is dry, opening windows helps remove moisture from indoor air, which helps prevent mold from growing. I recommend opening the windows for at least thirty minutes a week year-round *(and it could be for 10 minutes, 3 times a week)*.

Opening windows is not always an option, however. If outdoor air is warm or damp, if the outdoor environment is smoggy or smoky, or if it is pollen season, it is best to keep windows closed and run an air conditioner instead. Avoid opening windows on particularly windy days, when breezes can blow excessive amounts of pollen, mold spores, and dust into your home. Use window screens to keep bugs out, and be sure to run a damp cloth along windowsills to pick up any allergens or dust that have come in from outside.

Clean Design Ventilation Strategy #2
Run Air Conditioners

When outdoor air is unsuitable, running an air conditioner can bring cooler, dryer, filtered air into your home. Air conditioners remove some of the moisture and heat from outdoor air before blowing it in to your home.

To make sure your air conditioner pumps filtered, clear air into your home, be sure to replace filters often. How often? Use the manufacturer's recommendations as a guide, but check the filter more frequently and replace or clean it if it needs it. I suggest changing filters on air conditioners and heaters a minimum of every three months and consider using washable filters to be eco-friendly. Check all parts of the air conditioner or system and clean out any dirt, mold, or water that collects. In central air systems, be sure ducts, fans, and condenser units are cleaned and serviced regularly. This also will increase the efficiency of your furnace and save on energy costs. Run air conditioners with the vents set on "open" to bring outdoor air in. Closing vents causes indoor air to be recirculated, which can mean that you are perpetuating the "chemical stew" in your indoor air.

Q: WHAT ARE HEPA FILTERS, AND WHY SHOULD I USE THEM?

A: HEPA stands for "high-efficiency particulate air." HEPA filters are capable of removing small particles of pollen, dust, and other pollutants and allergens from the air. To meet HEPA standards, a filter must be 99.97 percent efficient in removing particles as small as 0.3 microns—which is pretty small. (A human hair is between 20 and 200 microns thick.) I recommend using these filters and HEPA-filter vacuums because they do an excellent job of cleaning the air. They can be more expensive than other products, but because they help protect your family's health, they are worth every penny.

Panasonic JetForce HEPA
filter vacuum

VENTILATION FOR HEATERS

Appliances and heaters that burn any kind of fuel, including space heaters, gas stoves, wood stoves, and fireplaces, must be properly ventilated because they produce gas, fumes, and airborne particles that pollute indoor air. For example, fuel-burning devices produce carbon monoxide and nitrogen dioxide, which are both colorless and odorless gases that can cause irritation of the respiratory tract and other symptoms. Be sure to follow the manufacturer's instructions when installing and using any fuel-burning devices.

Clean Design Ventilation Strategy #3
Run Exhaust Fans

An exhaust fan should be installed in bathrooms, kitchens, and other rooms that have humidity to reduce the growth of mold. Make sure built-in exhaust fans vent outside of your home and not into the attic, crawlspace, between walls, or into the basement. In the past some building codes allowed indoor venting, but it is a terrible idea because all it does is move humidity from one part of your home to another. An inexpensive way to manage indoor air quality is to use a window fan as an exhaust fan by turning it around to blow air out.

Clean Design Ventilation Strategy #4
Use Air Cleaners

Another option for cleaning indoor air is using an air purifier. These are sold as freestanding units or as components in central air and heating systems. If you use an air purifier, choose one that is energy-efficient and that uses HEPA filters. Is it worthwhile to spend hundreds or thousands of dollars buying and installing air cleaners in your home? Here is what the experts at the Asthma and Allergy Foundation of America (AAFA) have to say on this topic:

> "Although the EPA recommends air filtration, controlling the sources of allergy-causing pollution and ventilation are more important. Air cleaners are worth considering, but not as a solution to your asthma or allergy problems by themselves. In fact, research studies disagree on whether or not filters give much added relief in a clean and well-ventilated home.
>
> "While many allergens and irritants are suspended in household air, there are far more resting on surfaces like rugs, furniture, and countertops. Keeping these areas clean is an important step in controlling your allergy and asthma triggers. However, the most effective step is to eliminate the source of these allergens and irritants in the first place."[66]

So it really is up to you whether to use air cleaners. And definitely do not rely on them to take secondhand smoke out of a home with people who smoke indoors; no air filter can remove secondhand smoke in a safe and effective way. If someone in your home smokes, urge them to quit and forbid them to smoke in your house.

Clean Design Ventilation Strategy #5
Test for Radon

Radon is a radioactive gas that forms as a result of the natural breakdown of uranium in soil, water, and rock. It enters homes through openings or cracks in the floors or foundations, and is colorless, odorless, and tasteless. According to the EPA, radon exposure is responsible for an estimated 21,000 deaths from lung cancer each year.[67] Some neighborhoods are known to have higher levels of radon in general, but indoor radon rates can vary from one home to the next.

The best way to determine whether radon is present in your home is to perform a radon test. You can buy one at your local hardware store or home supply retailer, or you can hire a professional radon tester to conduct the sampling for you. If there are high levels of radon in your home, repairs and radon reduction systems can be used to reduce radon. New homes can be constructed with radon-reducing features; if you are building a new home, be sure to ask your architect for details. To find out more about radon, go to www.epa.gov/radon/.

CONCLUSION

Now that you know all the ins and outs of Clean Design, you can make decorating choices for every room in your home that will support your family's health and the health of the planet. You can help family members manage their allergy and asthma symptoms by eliminating and managing many of the allergens that trigger attacks, such as chemical fumes, mold, dust, pollen, odors, and airborne toxins. By following the principles of Clean Design, you can turn your home into a sanctuary for the people you love and create an allergen-reduced environment that nurtures good health.

Think of this book as the beginning of your education about Clean Design. There are many other excellent sources of information about what you can do to make your home safer for allergy and asthma sufferers and more eco-friendly. To learn more, please read some of the sources and articles recommended in the Selected Bibliography.

I also encourage you to view and bookmark the following two websites:

- Robin Wilson Home website (www.robinwilsonhome.com) to see our news segments, articles, social media, and blog, which provide advice and information of interest to people who share our excitement for wellness and a lifestyle focused on Clean Design.

- Review the Resource Guide (www.cleandesignbook.com) for this book.

NOTES

Introduction

1. Asthma and Allergy Foundation of America (AAFA), "Allergy Facts and Figures," http://www.aafa.org/display.cfm?id=9&sub=30.
2. American Lung Association, "Indoor Air Quality," http://www.lung.org/associations/charters/mid-atlantic/air-quality/indoor-air-quality.html.

Section I: Portraits of Clean Design: Ideas and Inspiration

Chapter 2: Living Rooms

3. Energy Star, "Standby Power and Energy Vampires," https://www.energystar.gov/index.cfm?c=about.vampires.
4. Ibid.

Chapter 3: Kitchens: Hearth of the Home

5. Environmental Protection Agency (EPA), WaterSense, "The WaterSense Label," http://www.epa.gov/WaterSense/about_us/watersense_label.html.
6. Energy Star, "Energy Star @ Home Tips," http://www.energystar.gov/index.cfm?c=products.es_at_home_tips.
7. Energy Star, "Best Practices: Refrigerators," https://www.energystar.gov/index.cfm?c=refrig.pr_best_practices_refrigerators.

Chapter 4: Bedrooms: One-Third of Your Life

8. Consumer Product Safety Commission, "Quantitative Assessment of Potential Health Effects from the Use of Fire Retardant (FR) Chemicals in Mattresses," January 9, 2006, https://www.cpsc.gov//PageFiles/88208/matttabd.pdf.
9. Deb Post Unplugged (blog), "What Are the Risks of Sleeping on a Chemically Treated Mattress?," February 20, 2013, http://www.debpost.com/2013.02.17_arch.html; GREENGUARD Environmental Institute, "Chemicals in Common Products: Risky Business for Children's Health," 2009, http://www.google.com/url?sa=t&rct=j&q=&esrc=s&source=web&cd=20&ved=0CFYQFjAJOAo&url=http%3A%2F%2Fwww.greenguard.org%2FLibraries%2FGG_Documents%2FReformat_GG_RiskyBusiness_1.sflb.ashx&ei=qMcmVK_1Fs2TyATkmYLYCw&usg=AFQjCNEgN3BvPPliTnf0QFHAiAnSlTyBEA&bvm=bv.76247554,d.aWw.
10. Centers for Disease Control and Prevention (CDC), "Are You Getting Enough Sleep?" updated April 14, 2014, http://www.cdc.gov/features/sleep/.
11. National Sleep Foundation, "Healthy Sleep Tips," http://sleepfoundation.org/sleep-tools-tips/healthy-sleep-tips.
12. Mayo Clinic, "Sleep Tips: 7 Steps to Better Sleep," http://www.mayoclinic.org/healthy-living/adult-health/in-depth/sleep/art-20048379.

Chapter 5: Baby Nursery

13. University of Texas, "Crib Mattresses Emit High Rates of Potentially Harmful Chemicals, Cockrell School Engineers Find," April 2, 2014, http://www.utexas.edu/news/2014/04/02/crib-mattresses-emit-chemicals/.
14. Ibid.
15. Ibid.
16. Ibid.
17. American Academy of Allergy, Asthma & Immunology (AAAAI), "Prevention of Allergies and Asthma: Tips to Remember," 2013, http://www.aaaai.org/conditions-and-treatments/library/at-a-glance/prevention-of-allergies-and-asthma-in-children.aspx.
18. CDC, "Secondhand Smoke and Asthma," updated May 9, 2014, http://www.cdc.gov/tobacco/campaign/tips/diseases/secondhand-smoke-asthma.html.
19. American Academy of Pediatrics, "Breastfeeding

Benefits Your Baby's Immune System,"
healthychildren.org, updated July 10, 2014, http://
www.healthychildren.org/English/ages-stages/baby/
breastfeeding/Pages/Breastfeeding-Benefits-Your-
Baby%27s-Immune-System.aspx.

20. American Academy of Pediatrics, "Breastfeeding
and the Use of Human Milk," *Pediatrics* 129:3, March
1, 2012, http://pediatrics.aappublications.org/
content/129/3/e827.full.

Chapter 6: Bathrooms

21. EPA, WaterSense, "Showerheads," http://www.epa
.gov/WaterSense/products/showerheads.html.

22. Ibid.

23. Ibid.

24. Center for Health, Environment & Justice, "What Is
That New Shower Curtain Smell?" http://chej.org/
campaigns/pvc/resources/shower-curtain-report/.

25. EPA, WaterSense, "Toilets," http://www.epa.gov/
watersense/products/toilets.html.

26. Ibid.

27. CDC, "Handwashing: Clean Hands Save Lives, How
Should You Wash Your Hands," http://www.cdc.gov/
handwashing/when-how-handwashing.html.

**Chapter 8: Laundry Rooms, Basements, Garages, and
Attics**

28. EPA, Green Building, "Laundry Room & Basement,"
December 19, 2012, http://www.epa.gov/greenhomes/
Basement.htm.

29. Ibid.

30. Ibid.

31. Energy Star, "Best Practices: Clothes Washer Tips,"
https://www.energystar.gov/index.cfm?c=
clotheswash.clothes_washers_performance_tips.

32. Energy Star, "Best Practices: Clothes Dryer Tips,"
https://www.energystar.gov/index.cfm?c=
clotheswash.clothes_washers_performance_tips.

33. EPA, "Learn About Chemicals Around Your House:
Moth Balls," http://www.epa.gov/kidshometour/
products/moth.htm.

Chapter 9: Outdoor Living

34. AAFA, Editorial Board, "Gardening with Allergies,"
http://www.aafa.org/display.cfm?id=9&sub=19&-
cont=470.

35. Ibid.

36. Ibid.

37. Ibid.

38. Adapted from Neil Osterwell, "Foods that May
Worsen Pollen Allergies," Web MD Allergies Health
Center, November 6, 2012, http://www.webmd.com/
allergies/features/oral-allergy-syndrome-foods.

39. AAFA, Editorial Board, "Ragweed Allergy," updated
2005, http://www.aafa.org/display.cfm?id=9&sub
=19&cont=267.

40. Ibid.

Section II: Wellness Guide to Clean Design

**Chapter 10: Clean Design: What It Is, and Why It
Matters**

41. Adapted from American Lung Association, "Indoor
Air Quality," http://www.lung.org/associations/char-
ters/mid-atlantic/air-quality/indoor-air-quality.html.

42. American Lung Association, "Indoor Air Quality,"
http://www.lung.org/associations/charters/mid-
atlantic/air-quality/indoor-air-quality.html.

43. AAFA, "Allergy Facts and Figures," http://www.aafa
.org/display.cfm?id=9&sub=30.

44. Ibid.

45. Ibid.

46. AAFA, Editorial Board, "Asthma Overview," updated
2005, http://www.aafa.org/display.cfm?id=8&cont=5.

47. Ibid.

48. Ibid.

49. EPA, "Frequently Asked Questions about
Drycleaning," http://www.epa.gov/dfe/pubs/garment/
ctsa/factsheet/ctsafaq.htm#5.

Chapter 11: Surfaces: Countertops, Walls, and Flooring

50. CDC, "Organic Solvents," updated December 30, 2013,
http://www.cdc.gov/niosh/topics/organsolv.

51. EPA, "An Introduction to Indoor Air Quality: Volatile
Organic Compounds," http://www.epa.gov/iaq/voc
.html.

52. Ibid.

53. Benjamin Moore, "About Green Promise Paints," http://www.benjaminmoore.com/en-us/for-your-home/green-promise-environmentally-friendly-paint.

54. Safer Chemicals, Healthy Families, "Health Report: Reproductive Health and Fertility Problems," http://saferchemicals.org/health-report/chemicals-and-our-health/reproduction/.

Chapter 12: Furniture and Furnishings

55. Chris Chamberlin, "Why Sleep on an Organic Mattress?" The Clean Bedroom, http://www.thecleanbedroom.com/Organic_Mattresses/organic_mattresses_and_toppers.html.

56. National Cancer Institute, "Fact Sheet: Formaldehyde and Cancer Risk," http://www.cancer.gov/cancertopics/factsheet/Risk/formaldehyde.

57. EPA, "An Introduction to Indoor Air Quality: Formaldehyde," http://www.epa.gov/iaq/formaldehyde.html.

58. National Cancer Institute, "Fact Sheet: Formaldehyde and Cancer Risk," http://www.cancer.gov/cancertopics/factsheet/Risk/formaldehyde.

Chapter 15: Cleaning Tools and Tips

59. AAFA, Editorial Board, "Dust Mites," updated 2005, http://www.aafa.org/display.cfm?id=9&sub=18&cont=228.

Chapter 16: Trigger Safe: How to Eliminate and Manage the Top Ten Allergy and Asthma Triggers

60. American Cancer Society, "Secondhand Smoke," February 11, 2014, http://www.cancer.org/cancer/cancercauses/tobaccocancer/secondhand-smoke.

61. Ibid.

62. CDC, "Mold: Basic Facts," updated May 22, 2014, http://www.cdc.gov/mold/faqs.htm.

63. P. F. Louis, "Beware of Hidden Toxin Sources in New Clothes," *Natural News*, September 1, 2012, http://www.naturalnews.com/037038_new_clothes_toxic_chemicals_washing.html.

64. EPA, "Frequently Asked Questions about Drycleaning," http://www.epa.gov/dfe/pubs/garment/ctsa/factsheet/ctsafaq.htm#5.

Chapter 17: Building Envelope: Healthier and Nontoxic Options

65. EPA, "Indoor Air Facts No.4: Sick Building Syndrome," http://www.epa.gov/iaq/pdfs/sick_building_factsheet.pdf.

66. AAFA, "Portable Air Cleaners," http://www.aafa.org/display.cfm?id=8&sub=16&cont=37.

67. EPA, "Health Risks—Report: EPA's Assessment of Risks from Radon in Homes," http://www.epa.gov/radon/risk_assessment.html.

SELECTED BIBLIOGRAPHY

The following is a list of articles and websites that provide trustworthy, useful information about designing a clean, healthy home environment:

Allergies

American Academy of Allergy, Asthma & Immunology (AAAAI), **"Allergies,"** http://www.aaaai.org/conditions-and-treatments/allergies.aspx.

AAAAI, **"Prevention of Allergy and Asthma in Children: Tips to Remember,"** http://www.aaaai.org/conditions-and-treatments/library/at-a-glance/prevention-of-allergies-and-asthma-in-children.aspx.

American Academy of Pediatrics, **"Allergy Tips,"** http://www.aap.org/en-us/about-the-aap/aap-press-room/news-features-and-safety-tips/pages/Allergy-Tips.aspx.

Asthma and Allergy Foundation of America (AAFA), **"Allergy Facts and Figures,"** http://www.aafa.org/print.cfm?id=9&sub=30.

Mayo Clinic, **"Allergy-Proof Your Home,"** http://www.mayoclinic.org/diseases-conditions/allergies/in-depth/allergy/art-20049365.

National Institute of Allergy and Infectious Diseases, **"Pollen Allergy,"** http://www.niaid.nih.gov/topics/allergicDiseases/understanding/pollenallergy/Documents/pllenAllergy.pdf.

National Library of Medicine Medline Plus, **"Allergic Reactions,"** http://www.nlm.nih.gov/medlineplus/ency/article/000005.htm.

Asthma

AAAAI, **"Asthma,"** http://www.aaaai.org/conditions-and-treatments/asthma.aspx.

AAAAI, **"Prevention of Allergies and Asthma in Children: Tips to Remember,"** http://www.aaaai.org/conditions-and-treatments/library/at-a-glance/prevention-of-allergies-and-asthma-in-children.aspx.

American Academy of Pediatrics, "**Asthma Triggers and What to Do About Them,"** http://www.healthychildren.org/English/health-issues/conditions/allergies-asthma/pages/Asthma-Triggers-and-What-to-do-About-Them.aspx.

American Lung Association, **"Reduce Asthma Triggers,"** http://www.lung.org/lung-disease/asthma/taking-control-of-asthma/reduce-asthma-triggers.html.

AAFA, **"Dust Mites,"** http://aafa.org/display.cfm?id=9&sub=18&cont=228.

Centers for Disease Control and Prevention (CDC), **"How is Asthma Treated?"** http://www.cdc.gov/asthma/management.html.

CDC, **"Secondhand Smoke and Asthma,"** last updated May 9, 2014, http://www.cdc.gov/tobacco/campaign/tips/diseases/secondhand-smoke-asthma.html.

Environmental Protection Agency (EPA), **"Asthma Triggers: Gain Control of Dust Mites,"** http://www.epa.gov/asthma/dustmites.html.

National Institute of Allergy and Infectious Diseases, **"Asthma Facts,"** http://www.niaid.nih.gov/topics/asthma/understanding/Pages/facts.aspx.

National Institutes of Health, **"Stay Away from Asthma Triggers,"** http://www.nlm.nih.gov/medlineplus/ency/patientinstructions/000064.htm.

Consumer Safety

Center for Health, Environment & Justice, **"What Is That New Shower Curtain Smell?"** http://chej.org/campaigns/pvc/resources/shower-curtain-report/.

EPA, **"Chromated Copper Arsenate (CCA): Consumer Safety Information Sheet: Inorganic Arsenical Pressure-Treated Wood,"** http://www.epa.gov/oppad001/reregistration/cca/cca_consumer_safety.htm.

EPA, **"Moth Balls,"** http://www.epa.gov/kidshometour/products/moth.htm.

Green America, **"Green Dry Cleaning,"** http://www.greenamerica.org/livinggreen/drycleaning.cfm.

Greenpeace, **"New Study Finds Toxic Monsters Lurking in Children's Clothing,"** http://www.greenpeace.org/international/en/press/releases/New-study-finds-toxic-monsters-lurking-in-childrens-clothing1/.

Healthy Child Healthy World, **"Reduce Your Use of PVC in Plastics and Other Household Products,"** February 22, 2013, http://healthychild.org/easy-steps/reduce-your-use-of-pvc-in-plastics-and-other-household-products/.

Louis, P.F. **"Beware of Hidden Toxin Sources in New Clothes,"** Natural News, September 1, 2012, http://www.naturalnews.com/037038_new_clothes_toxic_chemicals_washing.html.

National Cancer Institute, **"Formaldehyde and Cancer Risk,"** http://www.cancer.gov/cancertopics/factsheet/Risk/formaldehyde.

University of Texas at Austin, **"Crib Mattresses Emit High Rates of Potentially Harmful Chemicals, Cockrell School Engineers Find,"** April 2, 2014, http://www.utexas.edu/news/2014/04/02/crib-mattresses-emit-chemicals/.

Energy and Water Efficiency

Energy Star, **"How a Product Earns the Energy Star Label,"** https://www.EnergyStar.gov/certified-products/how-product-earns-label.

EPA, **"About Energy Star"** https://www.EnergyStar.gov/about/.

EPA, **"Toilets,"** http://www.epa.gov/WaterSense/products/toilets.html.

EPA, **"Water-Efficient Showerheads,"** http://www.epa.gov/WaterSense/products/showerheads.html.

U.S. Department of Energy, **"Where to Insulate in a Home,"** www.energy.gov/energysaver/articles/where-insulate-home.

U.S. Green Building Council, **"LEED,"** http://www.usgbc.org/leed.

Fire Safety

U.S. Fire Administration, **"Learn About Smoke Alarms,"** http://www.usfa.fema.gov/campaigns/smokealarms/alarms/index.shtm?utm_source=Twitter&utm_medium=Social%2BMedia%2BMarketing&utm_campaign=Status%2BUpdates.

General Health Issues

American Academy of Pediatrics, **"Breastfeeding Benefits Your Baby's Immune System,"** healthychildren.org, updated July 10, 2014, http://www.healthychildren.org/English/ages-stages/baby/breastfeeding/Pages/Breastfeeding-Benefits-Your-Baby%27s-Immune-System.aspx.

CDC, **"Are You Getting Enough Sleep?"** http://www.cdc.gov/features/sleep/.

National Cancer Institute, **"Harms of Smoking and Health Benefits of Quitting,"** http://www.cancer.gov/cancertopics/factsheet/Tobacco/cessation.

Greening Your Home

Care.com. **"Creating a Toxin-Free Home,"** http://www.care.com/housekeeping-creating-a-toxin-free-home-p1017-q14637.html.

EPA, **"A Citizen's Guide to Radon,"** http://www.epa.gov/radon/pubs/citguide.html.

EPA, **"Attic and Roof,"** http://www.epa.gov/greenhomes/attic.htm.

EPA, **"Laundry Room and Basement,"** http://www.epa.gov/greenhomes/Basement.htm.

Rysavy, Tracy Fernandez **"The Allergen-Free Bedroom,"** Green America, January/February 2006, http://www.greenamerica.org/livinggreen/bedrooms.cfm.

U.S. Green Building Council, **"Green Home Guide,"** http://greenhomeguide.com/askapro/question/i-m-moving-into-an-apartment-that-has-been-painted-with-a-voc-paint-what-can-i-do-including-repainting-to-reduce-my-exposure.

Indoor Air Quality

American Lung Association, **"Indoor Air Quality,"** http://www.lung.org/associations/charters/mid-atlantic/air-quality/indoor-air-quality.html.

American Lung Association, **"Keep Pollution Out of Your Home,"** http://www.lung.org/healthy-air/home/resources/keep-pollution-out-of-your-home.html#ventilate.

American Lung Association, **"10 Tips to Protect Yourself from Unhealthy Air,"** http://www.lung.org/healthy-air/outdoor/protecting-your-health/protecting-yourself/.

CDC, **"Indoor Air Quality Information,"** http://www.cdc
.gov/nceh/airpollution/indoor_air.htm.

EPA, **"Care for Your Air: A Guide to Indoor Air Quality,"**
http://www.epa.gov/iaq/pubs/careforyourair.html.

EPA, **"Guide to Air Cleaners In the Home,"** http://www
.epa.gov/iaq/pubs/airclean.html.

EPA, **"Indoor Air Facts No. 4: Sick Building Syndrome,"**
http://www.epa.gov/iaq/pdfs/sick_building_factsheet.pdf.

EPA, **"An Introduction to Indoor Air Quality: Volatile
Organic Compounds,"** http://www.epa.gov/iaq/voc.html.

Occupational Safety and Health Administration,
"Indoor Air Quality," https://www.osha.gov/SLTC/
indoorairquality/.

Mold

CDC, **"Facts About Mold and Dampness,"** http://www
.cdc.gov/mold/dampness_facts.htm.

EPA, **"Mold Resources,"** http://www.epa.gov/mold/
moldresources.html.

Florida Solar Energy Center, **"Mold Growth,"** http://www
.fsec.ucf.edu/en/consumer/buildings/basics/moldgrowth
.htm.

Paint and VOCs

Benjamin Moore, **"About Green Promise Paints,"** http://
www.benjaminmoore.com/en-us/for-your-home/green-
promise-environmentally-friendly-paint.

Better Homes & Gardens, **"The Chemistry of Paint,"**
DIYadvice, http://www.diyadvice.com/diy/painting/paint/
chemistry/.

EPA, **"Painting and Indoor Air Quality,"** http://www.epa
.gov/iaq/homes/hip-painting.html.

INDEX

walls, 49–50, 62, 74, 90, 121–22,
    124, 172
Sustainable Furnishings Council, 22,
    46, 137

T
tile floors, 129
tobacco smoke, 64, 112, 167–68, 183
toilets, 69, 71–72
Toxic Hot Seat (movie), 22
toys, 61–62
triggers. *See also* dust mites; mold
    air quality, 4, 110–12
    cleaning supplies, 58, 158, 176
    clothing, 175
    dust, 44–45, 49–50, 126, 143,
        148–49, 174
    elimination and management of,
        2–3, 5–7, 112–17, 167
    odors, 158, 177
    pet dander, 112, 139, 169
    pollen, 97–101, 102, 172–74
    summary, 2–3, 168
    tobacco smoke, 64, 112, 167–68
    vermin, 176–77
    wood smoke, 22, 103–5, 177

U
University of Texas at Austin, 58
upholstery and cushions, 22, 58, 136,
    138–39, 142, 160, 163–64
U.S. Energy Department, 93

V
vacuums, 63, 148, 181
ventilation, 32, 64, 69, 77–78, 79,
    123–24, 170–71, 179–83
vermin, 176–77
VOCs (volatile organic compounds).
    See also chemicals
    in floor finishes, 127–28
    in home offices, 80
    in mattresses, 58–59
    in paints, 62, 117, 121, 122
    in shower curtain liners, 70

sources of, 121
as triggers, 112

W
wallpaper, 50, 69, 170, 172
walls, 49–50, 62, 74, 90, 121–22, 124,
    172
washers, 41, 86–89, 160
water consumption, 36, 68–69,
    71–72, 86
water leaks, 69, 90, 92, 93, 148,
    171–72
WaterSense ratings, 36, 69
window treatments, 49, 62, 145–49
windows, 145–46, 148, 160, 180–81
wood. *See* floors; furniture
wood smoke, 22, 103–5, 177
wood stoves, 111, 177, 182

ABOUT THE AUTHOR

Robin Wilson is a nationally eco-friendly lifestyle brand and interior designer focused on designing beautiful, eco-friendly spaces and sharing her knowledge with consumers about wellness options she uses in her practice which she has called "Clean Design." She has spent the past fifteen years working on projects and advocating for clean construction and design methods through her eponymous design firm, Robin Wilson Home, based in New York City.

She is the first woman with a branded line of custom kitchen and bath cabinetry sold by over four hundred Holiday Kitchens independent dealers nationwide. She was first featured in Oprah's magazines, and her work has been featured in national press such as *House Beautiful*, *Elle Décor*, *Esquire*, *Essence*, the *New York Times*, and *Natural Homes & Gardens*, among others. Her design firm continues to handle select projects across the country. Her team has created and worked with clients of all budgets to create eco-friendly design projects, including EcoBungalow-LA, the Good Housekeeping Show House (Harlem), a penthouse for an HGTV "Selling New York" segment, the terrace at the Esquire Ultimate Bachelor Apartment, the White House Fellows Office, and several projects in the Harlem office of President Bill Clinton. Her firm also designs private homes and has consulted with an international hotel group. Named one of the Top 20 African American Designers, an Eco-Hero for Sustainable Design, and one of the *New York Post*'s 50 Most Powerful Women, Wilson is also a blogger for *Huffington Post*, where she writes about eco-health issues.

Since 2011, she has served as an ambassador for the Asthma and Allergy Foundation of America, where she helps increase awareness of indoor air quality issues that affect wellness in residential and commercial spaces.

She partnered in 2014 with consumer products giant Panasonic to promote their latest line of cutting-edge products for the home, which are both energy efficient and an integral part of a Clean Design strategy. And she is a member of the Board of the Sustainable Furnishings Council.

Having grown up enduring frequent hospitalizations for asthma and allergies, Wilson has a deep understanding of the challenges facing people with respiratory diseases. Wilson was a key part of the team that rebuilt the mold-ravaged private residence of environmentalist Robert F. Kennedy Jr., as documented in her book, *Kennedy Green House* (Greenleaf, 2010). In the book's foreword, Kennedy calls Wilson "an eco-friendly design pioneer." *Kennedy Green House* received the Bronze Award in the Home & Garden category from the Independent Publisher (IPPY) Book Awards.

The Robin Wilson Home licensed product line of bedding/bath products and hypoallergenic pillows is available through retailers such as Bed Bath & Beyond. Her furniture line, Nest Home by Robin Wilson, premiered in May 2013 at the International Contemporary Furniture Fair (ICFF) in New York City. She regularly appears on the speakers' circuit, on television, and offers commentary in print on design, wellness, sustainability, and allergy and asthma issues. She has a beautiful daughter and lives in the metro New York City area.

Alice Lesch Kelly is an award-winning, *New York Times* best-selling book collaborator, content marketing writer, and journalist specializing in health and wellness. She has co-authored ten consumer health books, and her feature articles have appeared in more than fifty magazines and newspapers, including the *New York Times*, the *Los Angeles Times, Martha Stewart Living, MORE,* and *O, the Oprah Magazine*. She lives in the Boston area with her family. Her website is www.AliceKelly.net.